shine:

embracing God's heart for you

AMY RIENOW

Kregel
Publications

Shine: Embracing God's Heart for You

© 2005 by Amy Rienow

Published by Kregel Publications, a division of Kregel, Inc., P.O. Box 2607, Grand Rapids, MI 49501.

Library of Congress Cataloging-in-Publication Data
Rienow, Amy.
Shine: embracing God's heart for you / by Amy Rienow.
    p. cm.
    1. Teenage girls—Religious life. I. Title.
BV4551.3.R54   2005
248.8'33—dc22   2005018601

ISBN 0-8254-3580-3

Printed in the United States of America

05 06 07 08 09 / 5 4 3 2 1

To my husband, Rob,
who has loved me like
Christ loves the church.
You are the greatest blessing
of my life.

Contents

Acknowledgments

Thanks to Dori Gough, for all the work that she did in the early days of this book; Deb Covell, for encouraging me, and more importantly for the model that she is in her service to high school girls; Laura McElwee, for being a great friend and prayer partner; my parents, John and Jean Diehl, who have always loved me unconditionally; and my children, RW, Lissy, JD, and Marlayna—God has used you to show me His heart for His children.

Finally, I want to thank the many girls and volunteer staff who have been a part of the Student Body ministry at Wheaton Bible Church. It has been a privilege serving Christ with you.

Introduction

Do You Shine?

God created you to shine. Do you believe it?

For many of us, being a Christian is something we naturally fell into. It wasn't something that we studied hard for . . . like we would before a big chemistry test. Christianity is the view of the world that we grew up with. For example, we grew up accepting the truth that God created the world. We looked up to childhood heroes and were told that Jesus is the best hero of all. We were loved by our family and were taught that God loves us more than anyone else.

Not everyone grows up with this basic belief in Christianity. Many girls find faith in Christ in their teen years and develop a relationship with God apart from any family influence. Still, the truths of Christianity can become so routine that they're no different than the stuff we learn about in social studies.

When my son RW was three years old, we were driving in the car when he said, "Mom, I have a great idea! Let's go to Disney World . . . and . . . we can see . . . JESUS!" I kept from laughing, and then I responded, "That is a great idea. But did you know that we can see Jesus right now because He's always with us?" RW answered with a flat, "Oh."

My response was obviously not as exciting to him as the idea of going to Disney World. What a perfect example of what sometimes happens in our relationship with Jesus. In my son's mind, Jesus seemed to be a superhero, like Buzz Lightyear. So if Buzz Lightyear lived at Disney World, Jesus must live there too. My son was soaking in everything about God and Jesus that we were telling him, but was he distinguishing the truth of Jesus from the stories he'd heard about other heroes?

Our own responses to God can become like RW's. We've heard again and again that God loves us and we say, "Oh." We've heard that God has a plan for our lives and we say, "Oh." We've heard that God will never leave us and we say, "Oh."

The truth about God can be something we simply *accept as truth* or something we *believe*. There's a big difference. For example, let's look at the beliefs of Christopher Columbus. Most of the people of his time accepted as truth that the world was round. Yet sailors were still afraid to sail past the horizon of the Atlantic Ocean. Columbus was different. Because Columbus believed the world was round, he had the courage to sail west. He *believed* that the world was round and then *acted* in accordance with his *belief*. Many accepted as truth that the world was round, but they still just sat on the shores. By acting on his beliefs, Columbus earned a place in history.

We can just *accept as truth* that God loves us, that He has a plan for our lives, and that He'll never leave us or forsake us. But when we do, the truths about God and our relationship with Him become no different than the truths we accept about the world around us. We are simply "accepting as truth" ideas that an atheist would not accept as truth.

John 3:16 does not read, "For God so loved the world that He gave His one and only Son, that whoever *accepts as truth* this fact will be saved." No, John 3:16 says that whoever *believes* in Him will be saved. Believing in something is different from merely being able to accept it as truth. Believing requires active faith and trust.

Like Columbus, we have to take our own journey in order to prove these beliefs to ourselves. And although we may not earn any place in the history books, acting on our beliefs will certainly change the course of our own personal histories.

At the end of my college years I began to realize that I'd been merely accepting the truths about God. I accepted that God loved me, but believing it was different. One evening as I sat on my bed in my sorority bedroom, my knees curled up to my chest, I listened to a Christian song that I'd heard a hundred times. I felt afraid and trapped in my situation. I didn't want to end my engagement . . . even though I knew it was falling apart.

Suddenly the words of the song became crystal clear: "You know all my hopes and You know all my fears." I heard God speak to my heart, "Do you believe that I know your hopes and fears?" I experienced instant peace as my heart resonated with the truth about God. What I'd always *said* was true, I now *believed* in my own heart. I *believed* that God had a plan for me when all my earthly plans had crumbled.

Please understand that I had loved God since I was a child. As a little girl I had such a close relationship with God that I became upset because I couldn't hug Him. I not only loved Him with my whole heart, I also felt love from Him. I never doubted His love for me. I felt like I was God's favorite child, and that He had such special plans for me.

Adolescence, though, is the acute stage of life. Acute means "severe and intense." If you have a bad cold, for example, with a fever and a headache and you can't breathe through your nose, this is called the acute stage of the illness. After the acute stage has passed, you may still have a cough or a runny nose, but these symptoms will subside over time as you gradually get better. Adolescence is the acute stage of life. It's life at some of its most severe and intense. (There will be other acute times of life also, so it's not smooth sailing after adolescence!)

Any young woman in high school today would probably agree that her life is severe and intense. In adolescence most girls begin to struggle with their feelings about themselves, their relationships with others, and their relationships with their families. Girls may become entangled in sexual activity, eating disorders, stressed relationships with their parents, using alcohol or drugs, or rebelling against authority. The habits that are picked up in adolescence can be of long duration; in fact, they can take hold of us and carry on into our adult lives.

Many of you will say, "I don't smoke or drink, I'm certainly not having sex, I don't have a stressed-out relationship with my parents, and I'm not starving myself . . . so I must be okay." If this is what you're thinking then please read the following. I had the model, Christian girl, high-school life. I didn't drink or smoke, I didn't have sex with anyone, and I didn't engage in any sexual activity other than French kissing. I didn't have an eating disorder, and I had a good relationship with my parents (although, for the record, it was at times severe and intense). I didn't rebel against authority, but instead was admired by my teachers and principals. I had great friends, I was involved in all the "right" activities, and I was in leadership in my church youth group.

From the outside, everything looked great. But deep down certain habits were gaining a stronghold and I would drag those habits into adulthood. Somewhere along the way I had lost my childhood beliefs about who I was in God.

My prayer for all of you is that you begin to *believe* the truth about God and His Word . . . and shine!

In this study, we'll examine three parts that are involved in believing the truths of God. The first part is our heads (by this I mean our minds, not hair color). We'll look at what we now *accept* as truth and what it means to *believe* God's truth with our minds.

The second part is our hearts. We'll discover that it's one thing to understand our identities in Christ, and another to *believe* that Christ can be trusted with our identities.

Finally we will learn what it means to practice our faith with our hands. We will see that understanding the truth and believing in the truth is not enough to shine for God. We must also *do* the truth.

2 Timothy 3:1–7 will be the theme passage for our study. It reads,

> But mark this: There will be terrible times in the last days.
> People will be lovers of themselves, lovers of money, boastful,
> proud, abusive, disobedient to their parents, ungrateful,
> unholy, without love, unforgiving, slanderous, without self-

control, brutal, not lovers of the good, treacherous, rash, conceited, lovers of pleasure rather than lovers of God—having a form of godliness but denying its power. Have nothing to do with them.

They are the kind who worm their way into homes and gain control over weak-willed women, who are loaded down with sins and are swayed by all kinds of evil desires, always learning but never able to acknowledge the truth.

The Living Bible translates verse 5, "They will go to church, yes, but they won't really believe anything they hear," and verse 7, "Women of that kind . . . never understand the truth." We do not want to be weak-willed women who never understand the truth or believe the truth. We want to embrace a strong-willed approach to life, and the time to begin is right now. We as women don't have to be entrapped by sins or swayed by evil desires. Instead, we can become strong-willed women who seek freedom in the Lord.

This study has been brought about by two important influences. The first is my own experience. Everything I've written in this study comes from the Holy Spirit's conviction in my own life. Not every *example* I use comes from my own personal experience, but all the ideas in this study are the result of my spiritual journey. I'm still on this journey and don't plan on reaching my destination until I am home in heaven. So as you work through this study, don't be disillusioned and think that I've mastered my spiritual life.

The second influence is my experience as a youth-pastor's wife. I had a Holy Spirit–driven desire to begin Bible study groups to help young women come to embrace God's truth in their lives. I've seen Christian girls entangled in bad relationships with guys, suffering with eating disorders, drug and alcohol problems, and depression and anxiety.

In my heart of hearts, I knew that many of these problems were primarily spiritual in nature. Therefore, this study is an effort to help young Christian women not only free themselves from destructive behaviors, but to see themselves from God's perspective. Some of our problems are very big, and some may seem trivial in the grand scheme of things. But God is concerned with all the details of our lives, and it's in the little details that we often begin to experience His love for us. So my hope is that this material helps you to develop spiritual strength for breaking through whatever struggles you may encounter along your way.

Belief in God may be something we have fallen into naturally, but we have to act on our beliefs in order to grow in our relationship with Jesus Christ. My aim is that by the end of this book you'll shine for God like you never have before.

Believe with Your Head

Understanding God's Truth

1

The World Around Us

Shine Like a Star

If you have not chosen the kingdom of God, it will make in the end no difference what you have chosen instead.

—William Law

Have you ever had the feeling that you just don't belong?

Have you ever felt that you were different from your friends, your acquaintances, or even the people just walking past you on the street? Have you ever walked into a room and wanted to turn around and walk out because you believed that you just didn't fit in?

If you answered *yes* to any of these questions—congratulations! Yes, I congratulate you! If you've ever felt that you were an alien in a strange world, or a square in a room of circles, then you're on the right track. God did not create you to fit in. He created you to shine like a star in the universe!

- Look up Philippians 2:15, please, and write it below.

_____

_____

_____

God created you to shine like stars in this crooked and depraved generation. We were never supposed to "match" with the world around us. Just as every snowflake is unique, every person is unique. God created each snowflake, and God created you.

JD is my three-year-old son, and one of his favorite shows is the *Veggie Tales* children's series. JD sings the theme song every time we're at the grocery store or chopping vegetables for dinner, but he's also learning a very important biblical truth. At the end of every episode, Larry and Bob give the same simple message: ". . . and remember kids, God created you special and He loves you very much." Such incredible truth out of the mouths of a cucumber and a tomato! God created you special and He has a unique plan for your life.

Traps

As Christian women, we sometimes fall into three traps:

- **Trap 1:** We never feel different from the world around us and actually strive to fit in.
- **Trap 2:** We feel out of place and assume that the feeling means there's something wrong with us.
- **Trap 3:** We become so accustomed to the feeling of being different from others that we excel in it—and make ourselves so different that we have very little in common with others.

What do these traps look like when they're lived out?

The In Crowd

Trap number one is usually Satan's plan for those of us who pretty easily fit in with the crowd. We have a fairly easy time conforming to the world's standards of what a young woman should be like, and we put on that persona. In other words, we can speak, act, and dress the part and, from an external perspective at least, we do it with ease. We know what it takes to fit into "The Group," and we embrace our social role in life. We also get a lot of positive feedback about the persona we're wearing and become very comfortable wearing it. We become so comfortable that we no longer have the desire or need to take any risks. We can live in this world and feel fairly secure.

The result of this trap is a mind-set that's focused on belonging to the world and not to Christ. We've exchanged our uniqueness in Christ for the sameness of those around us. The result is a star whose light is dim in the universe.

Outside Looking In

Trap number two is Satan's scheme for those of us who feel rather insecure about our ability to connect with those around us. We feel that we've tried to fit in but, for whatever reason, continually fail. Therefore, something must be wrong with us.

We search for the culprit in ourselves. Is it my hair? My personality? My family? My clothes? After trying different personal changes and still not succeeding in our attempts to belong, we usually resign ourselves to being "different" and accept it. This resignation is based, though, on the unfortunate belief that there's something wrong with us, and we just accept that too. Instead of joyfully embracing our God-given unique-ness, we resign ourselves to our differentness. The result is a star whose light is flickering in the universe.

Outside the Mold (and Fine, Thank You)

Trap number three is Satan's plan for those of us who realize we don't fit the common mold. Although we may have felt hurt at times because of our differentness, we boldly accept our uniqueness and wear it proudly as a badge. Often this badge of pride covers wounds such as feelings of rejection, but the badge prevents our insecurity from being revealed.

We cling to our uniqueness as the *source* of our security. And as we celebrate not fitting in, we become more convinced that we've nothing in common with those who aren't like us. Satan has once again distorted our God-given uniqueness and convinced us to proudly embrace our differentness. We do not boast in Christ, but we boast in our uniqueness. The result is a star whose light is distorted in the universe.

It would better illustrate these traps if names and personal stories were attached to them. So meet Melissa, Ashley, and Tracy. Melissa comes from a very loving Christian family. Her parents have always shown her love and approval from the time she was a little girl. Melissa has an easy time making friends. She's the type of girl who everyone—both boys and girls—wants to be friends with. In high school, she's involved in many activities and is the president of her class. She's considered intelligent by her teachers and peers, and she gets good grades.

All in all, Melissa seems to have everything going for her—from the world's perspective. Melissa has so much approval from the world, she has no need to be dependent on approval from Christ. While Melissa is supposed to shine out among her peers as a follower of Christ, she really can't risk standing out too much or she may lose her praise from the world. She will continue to be a nice, popular person, but when people are around Melissa they are primarily drawn to Melissa not to God. The light of her star is dim, not fulfilling the role God has for her, but instead blending into the world's design for success.

• Look up Romans 12:2, please, and write it in the lines below.

_____

_____

• According to this verse, what is the primary problem with Melissa's view of life?

_____

_____

_____

Now meet Ashley. Ashley also comes from a loving Christian home and has always had the approval of her parents. Ashley, though, has never had an easy time at school. Being a little on the chubby side, she can hardly remember a time when she didn't feel unable to measure up to the beautiful princess in the fairy tale—or even to her petite best friend, who always looks cute in anything she wears. Ashley has had good friends, but she's also acquainted with feelings of rejection and betrayal. No one would accuse her of being the life of the party, and no one notices if she can't make it to the movie on Friday night. The phone doesn't ring that much for her, and she wonders, *If I stopped calling others, would anyone ever call me?* Her feelings of rejection by the world overwhelm any sense of acceptance or love from God. She can't imagine that God wants her to shine for Him in the universe when she can't even feel comfortable in gym class. Timid and insecure, the light from her star flickers.

• Read Psalm 139:14, please, and write it in the lines below.

_____

_____

_____

• According to this verse, what is a major problem with which Ashley is struggling?

_____

_____

_____

Finally, meet Tracy. Tracy comes from what we wouldn't call a "good home." Her parents divorced when she was six, and since then her life has never been the same. Even now, she questions whether she was to blame for her parents' breakup, and she doesn't feel approval from her father, who's stopped seeing her. Tracy has always felt different than others in school and has never been very popular. She has always been teased for one thing or another. Tracy found some friends in junior high who seemed to understand her, and they accepted her for who she was . . . or who they thought she was. She grew a tough exterior that rejected others before others could reject her. She dyed her hair and dressed in ways that would draw attention on her terms. Tracy definitely stands out and is able to stand up for herself, but she doesn't shine for God because she's focused on shining for herself. The light from her star is distorted.

- Read Philippians 3:3, please, and write it in the lines below.

  _____

  _____

  _____

  _____

- According to this verse, what is a struggle that Tracy is having?

  _____

  _____

  _____

  _____

Go back and read the three traps again, and then answer the following questions:

- Do you see yourself falling into any of these traps?

  _____

  _____

  _____

- Do you fall into only one, or can you see yourself in different traps at different times?

  _____

  _____

  _____

  _____

- Now read 1 John 5:19. According to this verse, which of the following four choices are the two truths that we should be aware of?

    1. We are children of God.
    2. God loves the ways of the world.
    3. The world is under God's control.
    4. The world is under the control of the Evil One.

The answers are numbers 1 and 4—we are children of God, and the world is under the control of Satan. God is, of course, sovereign and nothing happens that He has not allowed to happen. But until Christ's return, Satan has a number of days during which the world is under his influence.

For the rest of this chapter, then, our study will focus on the second truth of 1 John 5:19, that the whole world is under the power and control of the Evil One. In the next chapter we'll focus on the truth that we are God's children.

- What do you think it means when the Bible says that the world is under the control of Satan?

_____

_____

_____

_____

We learn something interesting by looking at the original Greek word that the New International Version translates as "control." The word is *keimai* and it means "to lie or be laid with." What this verse is saying, then, is that the world is "in bed with the Devil." Every part of human culture is under the influence of Satan. The world's definitions of happiness, success, and fulfillment are intimately connected to the Evil One.

Worldly Messages

Take a look at the following list. This list doesn't include everything, but it gives an idea about how we're bombarded with Satan's messages about . . .

- how we should look and how much importance we should place on our appearance.
- how we should dress.
- whose opinions we should care about.
- what's considered intelligent and what is considered ignorant.
- what kind of life is deemed valuable or deemed not valuable.
- who we should respect and admire.
- what we should strive for.
- how to achieve happiness.
- the definition of a successful life.

Human wisdom, human intelligence, and human perspective are all under the influence of Satan. Try not to misunderstand the meaning of 1 John 5:19. John is not stating that everything that comes from human creation is evil. God has used humans, from Abraham to Paul, to make His truth well known. God also uses non-Christians to discover and reveal truth. The following statement is so worth remembering that it needs to be all in capital letters: ALL TRUTH IS GOD'S TRUTH. It doesn't matter who discovers it, truth belongs to God.

But John's point is that the one who is influencing the world at this point in history believes that his number-one job is to distort God's truth. That statement is also worthy to be printed in all capitals! SATAN'S PLAN IS TO DISTORT GOD'S TRUTH. There is a Father of Truth and a Father of Lies. The former can never be deceitful and the latter will not be truthful.

In Satan's world, he determines what is considered pretty or beautiful. In God's world, He created all people in the image of Himself. God has

Beauty Distorted	Beauty Revealed
In Satan's World • Beauty is focused on the external. • Today, this often means becoming thin to the point of starvation and even the rejection of a woman's body for a girl's body.	*In God's World* • Beauty begins with the fear of the Lord (Prov. 31), which puts the focus on the internal. • This means recognizing that women are a unique and special part of God's creation and created in His image.
Result • More than ever, women do not look like the media ideals. • Many women suffer from eating disorders or even destructive behavior to "correct themselves" (for example, heroin-addicted models). • Women spend a huge amount of their time and energy focused on themselves and, therefore, they are ineffective for Christ's kingdom. • In our society, men become attracted to girls, leading to a devaluing of women and to child pornography.	*Result* • Women are focused on serving God and will bring glory to Him as opposed to themselves. • Women possess freedom to be the women God created them to be. • Women understand their beauty as they see it reflected in the eyes of God. • Women can spend significantly more energy on God's kingdom and as a result will be blessed.

never created anything ugly, therefore everyone is beautiful. But Satan has influenced the world to evaluate people by certain standards and place labels on what is pretty and attractive.

So when a woman says, for example, "I'm not attractive," she's really saying, "According to Satan's rules, I don't fit the definition of attractive." This woman actually makes a choice to live by Satan's rules and, therefore, acts like a slave to his world. Do you think it's a coincidence that what Satan has elevated as attractive and beautiful often leads to self-destruction?

It may be easy to see the contrast between these two worlds when looking at the list on page 27. Yet on a daily basis many of us make the unfortunate choice to live in Satan's world instead of God's world. We live by the rules of the Evil One as opposed to the rules of the Righteous One.

• Read Romans 8:19–21.

• What does this verse say that the creation (or the world) is waiting for?

_____

_____

_____

The creation is waiting for the sons and daughters of God to be revealed and to be brought into the glorious *freedom* of the children of God. The world is waiting for you—daughters of Christ—to live in freedom, to bring God's rules of righteousness and truth into this world of decay and bondage.

What a glorious calling we have! When we live according to God's truth we benefit ourselves and bring hope to those around us. I surely want to live up to this calling. Do you?

We may understand the truth that Christ came to save us from the laws of sin. But do we understand the truth that Satan has a far-reaching impact on this world? The world around you is enslaved to sin. The people around you who do not know Christ are enslaved to sin, and the Christians around you may be living according to Satan's rules as opposed to

God's truth. I followed Satan's rules for a long time, even though I have been a Christian for as long as I can remember. But now I'm determined to seek God's ways in this corrupt world.

- What does Ecclesiastes 11:5 tell us about God's ways?

_____

_____

_____

God's ways are not always easy to determine, but He is faithful to show us His path as we seek Him. He will never mislead us as we daily seek to know Him.

The Road Too Often Taken

Imagine that when you become a Christian, God gives you a brand new car. The license plate is labeled COG 97 (Child of God in the year 1997). God tells you that He has an exciting journey planned for you, with plenty of fun and exciting adventures. You'll meet a lot of people along the way who will influence your journey.

God warns you, though, that you must be very attentive on your journey. You have to be alert, and you cannot daydream, doze off at the wheel, or take unnecessary detours. It's very easy to get lost, but He has given you a map (His Word), which you must refer to daily. This map will enable you to stay on track even if you miss some of the road signs along the way.

You don't focus on the road, though, as well as you should. You find yourself daydreaming at the wheel, and before you realize what's happening, you sometimes fall asleep. When you wake up, you don't quite know where you are. You sometimes take your own detours.

Before you know it, you're confused and you don't know which way to go. So what do you do? You do the most easy and natural thing—you stop and ask for directions. You head in the direction you've been told, and you see a lot of other cars on this road. You say, "This looks promising," or "This looks like I'm heading the right way." Soon you see more cars and you follow them. You think, "They must know where they're going."

All the other cars seem directed, and heading to a clear destination. Before you know it, you're on a highway traveling seventy miles an hour—a part of the pack. You don't know where you're going but you feel like you must be headed in the right direction. After all, all of these people can't be wrong.

So now you're in your car, license plate COG 97, just another member of the pack. You notice other license plates, and most of them say COW (Child of World) on them. And then it hits you—that sense of anxiety that you're going the wrong way. You're on the road of the world, not the road to glory. And now you're going so fast, you don't see a way to get off.

> Enter through the narrow gate. For wide is the gate and broad
> is the road that leads to destruction, and many enter through
> it. But small is the gate and narrow the road that leads to life,
> and *only a few find it.*
>
> —Matthew 7:13–14, emphasis added

How long do you want to be on that road? Do you want to spend a year there? Or maybe five years as you get through college? Or will it be ten or twenty years? Remember, though, the longer you're on this highway, the harder it will be to get off. Exits may become fewer and farther between, or you may become so comfortable at this pace, speeding along with all the other cars, that getting off seems too scary.

We were never intended to be traveling on the world's highway in our COG car. God gave us our car so we could follow His road.

I've spent time on the wrong highway. There are many different roads from which to choose—the drugs and alcohol route, the rebellion route, the people-pleaser route, and a host of others. God had to do some serious shouting to let me know that I was taking the wrong road.

It's so easy to become deceived, to become trapped on the wrong expressway. That's because even when we're on a highway of the world, we're still in our Christian car. We can use the cell phone to stay in contact with our Christian friends, we have our Bible road maps lying on the seat next to us, we regularly whiz by a church—all the right answers are close at hand. But because we're not paying attention, we head right on down the wrong highway, taking our cues from everyone around us, but never taking the time to look at our road maps. Each of us is simply a child of God following the way of the world.

It's exciting that God has a unique route for each of us. No one else, not even other Christians, are supposed to be on your road. It's yours alone—God wants to free you, to lead you to the exit ramp off the wrong highway and onto your own unique journey. This journey will include His hand-picked tour guides for your life. With His Word and His body of believers, He will reveal His exciting plans for you—plans that are different from those of everyone else in the world. Do you want to find out what that journey has in store for you? I know I do!

Student Testimony

I used to feel that the Bible was pretty outdated and old fashioned. Then, partly through my experience in this Bible study, it came alive to me. I learned that even though the Bible did not come right out and talk about eating disorders, God's Word had a lot to say to me about my life here and now. I learned that for every decision that I have to make, I could turn to God's Word as the manual for how to live the best life.

In the same way that lots of guys think they have to be tough and macho, girls often think they need to be thin and popular. As I looked into God's Word I found out that this whole way of thinking was way off base. In thinking about all of this I have come to realize that popularity, thinness, and coolness can be idols in people's lives. They are not the kind of idol that we make out of wood and bow down to, but we do sacrifice things for them and they control our lives.

I realized that as I was faced with all the issues in my life with family, friends, guys, and more, the only place I could turn was God. Jesus is the one who made me, and the potter understands everything about his clay. I am that clay, and He is molding me into a woman after His own heart. I now know that in order to be transformed by His love, I need to let His truth sink deeply into my heart. I know that being the woman that God has made me to be will not be easy, but it is my heart's desire, and I am thankful that Jesus will never give up on me, and that He has provided me with a church filled with people who will pray for me and support me no matter what.

Are you ready to shine like a star in the universe? From now on, let's strive to embrace our uniqueness in Christ and begin to add light to a dark world.

2

The Child Within Us

The Real You

Nobody can make you feel inferior without your permission.
—Eleanor Roosevelt

I hope the first chapter excited you and challenged you to seek out God's special plan for your life. You are the daughter of the most powerful King that ever has or will ever exist! In this chapter we'll focus on doing two important things:

1. Discovering what it means to have our identities in Christ.
2. Learning to trust Christ with our identities.

Growing Up Christian

Many of you who are going through this study probably come from a background similar to mine. I was raised in the church and accepted Christ at a very young age. I have, in fact, no memory of *not* believing in Him. As a child, I was so in love with Jesus and wished desperately that He could become flesh and blood so I could hug Him. I've always known Him as my Savior.

Therefore, by the time I was in high school and college I was well aware of my identity in Christ list (see pages 37–38). This list told me all the privileges I had as a daughter of the King of the universe. I would read and reread this list over and over, knowing in my head that everything the Bible said was true.

There was one problem. Every time I read the list, I had the same emotional response: "So what?" So what if I'm beautiful in Christ? Why don't I have a boyfriend? So what that I'm a new creation in Christ? I don't feel that way when I'm struggling with the same problems every day. So what if Christ died for me? Didn't He die for everyone? Despite all my efforts, and although I accepted all the items on the list to be the truth, it didn't make any difference in my daily life.

Maybe as you're reading this, you resonate with "So what?" Maybe you don't even know what the identity in Christ list is. If you've never discovered all the benefits of knowing Jesus Christ as your Savior then you'll be excited to learn about the identity God offers you. And if you can't see the daily benefits of *your* identity in Christ, we'll learn together how each of us can trust Christ with our identities.

- Reread, please, 1 John 5:19. Which two of these four options does this passage tell us are true?

  1. We are children of God.
  2. God loves the ways of the world.
  3. The world is under God's control.
  4. The world is under the control of the Evil One.

You probably remembered from chapter 1 that the answers are 1 and 4. We are children of God. That's the truth. And as the verse reads, we know that we are children of God.

> We know that we are children of God, and that the whole world is under the control of the evil one.
>
> —1 John 5:19

We have to *accept as truth* and *believe* that we are children of God. These two things are written separately because they are two different things. It's one thing to be able to say, "I understand that Christ died on the cross for me, and that if I accept Him as my savior I can become a child of God." But we can "understand" who we are in Christ without actually *believing* it.

The word *believe* has been somewhat diminished from its original meaning in Scripture. The Greek word *pistis* is translated into English interchangeably as either "belief" or "faith" and is used in the New Testament over five hundred times. But when the Bible talks about "believing God" or "having faith in God" it is never passive. Believing in God always means action.

Belief in Scripture, then, has to do not only with our heads, but also with our hearts and our hands. We need to believe in our heads who Jesus is and what He promised us in His Word. We need to believe with our hands by serving Him and by following His commandments. And most importantly we need to believe with our hearts by trusting Him with our lives. This is tough to do!

- Take time now and read 2 Timothy 3:1–7 (the theme passage of our study). Describe in your own words the meaning of verse 7.

  _____

  _____

  _____

I've been convicted time and again by verse 7: "Always learning but never able to acknowledge the truth." *Acknowledge* in this verse means "to confirm, endorse, ratify, or to practice." It conveys a sense of movement, such as to be able to practice the truth or walk in it. Understanding the truth is not enough to develop a close relationship with Jesus Christ; we have to acknowledge, or walk in—that is, act in—the truth if we want to experience freedom in Christ.

Let me illustrate this point with an example. Every one of us has parts of ourselves that we like and dislike. I was born with stubby, light eyelashes. As a result, when I started wearing makeup in junior high (and makeup is never very pretty in junior high), I became too fond of mascara. I used to read the silly questions in teen magazines like, "If you could only wear one type of makeup, what would it be?" My answer was always mascara. I began to think that I couldn't be seen without it. I felt unacceptable if I wasn't wearing mascara. God's Word says, though, that I'm accepted by Him (Rom. 15:7). I understood that God accepted me with and without mascara, but I didn't *act* according to this truth.

When I was in my early twenties, I began testing some of God's basic truths in my daily activities. At one point, I felt that He was calling me to give up mascara for a while. When I did so, I was trusting that I was acceptable even without mascara. If I was acceptable simply because God's Word said that I was accepted by Him, shouldn't I be able to accept myself? This was such a freeing experiment, because as I gave up mascara and found that no one else seemed to notice or treat me any differently, I realized that mascara wasn't that important. Instead of just understanding God's truth, I was actively walking in it.

Wearing mascara is not, of course, a wrong or a sinful desire (yes, I'm wearing it right now). I wanted to give you an example of the difference between understanding your identity in Christ versus actively trusting Christ with your identity, that is, trusting Christ with who you are.

We often think we need Christ-plus-something to feel good about who we are. In my example it was Christ-plus-mascara. Many things, though, could be put into that equation—Christ plus a boyfriend, Christ plus good grades, or Christ plus recognition. But these types of efforts to feel good about ourselves are misguided. They go back to Satan's rules about what's necessary to feel good about our identities. Living according to Satan's rules, however, can lead us into being controlled by our desires as opposed to being controlled by Christ.

Look again at 2 Timothy 3:6, which in the New Living Translation reads,

They are the kind who work their way into people's homes and win the confidence of vulnerable women who are burdened with the guilt of sin and controlled by many desires.

I've often been that vulnerable woman, burdened with the guilt of my sin and controlled by many desires. This is not the woman God wants me to be, and it's not who I want to be.

- How have you been burdened by the guilt of sin and controlled by many desires? Take some time to pray, and ask God to reveal to you the answer to this question.

_____

_____

_____

_____

Below are listed just a small number of the infinite blessings that we have as children of God.[1] These statements aren't how we'd normally describe ourselves. But they come directly from God's Word, and it's helpful to see what God says about us. As you read this list, ask yourself if you truly believe these things.

- I am the light of the world (Matt. 5:14).
- I am Christ's chosen friend (John 15:15).
- The Lord is my Shepherd, I have everything I need (Ps. 23:1).
- I am chosen and appointed by Christ to bear His fruit (John 15:16).
- I am one of God's holy people (Eph. 1:4).
- I have an inheritance from God (Eph. 1:14).
- I have been blessed with every spiritual blessing (Eph. 1:3).
- I am created in the image of God (Gen. 1:27).

---

1. For a more comprehensive list, see Neil T. Anderson, *Bondage Breaker* (Eugene, Ore.: Harvest House Publishers, 1990), 42–45.

- I am holy, and dearly loved (Col. 3:12).
- I have incredibly great power from God (Eph. 1:19).
- I have a wonderful future (Eph. 1:18).
- I am precious, honored, and loved (Isa. 43:4).

If you do not believe the truth about who you are as a child of God, you are destined to be vulnerable and controlled by your many desires. This, of course, makes you less effective in God's kingdom.

In order to further examine the principle of believing in God's truth, we'll take a look at a biblical figure who has a lot in common with us. Mary, the mother of Jesus, was around fourteen or fifteen years of age when God revealed the incredible journey He had planned for her life. Let's look at Mary from a fresh perspective.

The Story of Mary

The story of Mary is one of the first Bible stories that we were ever told. Every year at Christmas, we hear again the story about the young girl who was visited by an angel, was overshadowed by the Holy Spirit, and conceived the Son of God. The story has become so familiar to many of us that we can't imagine how God could teach us anything new through this passage. That's what I thought until God opened my eyes to how Mary's story may be more of my story than I ever considered. I think it's unlikely that I'll experience an immaculate conception, but I may be asked to believe in Him just like Mary did two thousand years ago.

Read Mary's story in Luke 1:26–56.

Let's first dispel some myths that may keep us from understanding how significant this passage can be for us today.

Myth 1: It Was Fairly Common for Angels to Appear to People

As you read that myth in print it may sound ridiculous. It's easy, though, to fall into the "Bible-time mind-set." You know what I mean—thinking that miracles happened all the time back then. "Oceans must have been parted frequently," we might say, "because I've read about it twice in the Bible, but I've never seen it happen today. God spoke clearly through dreams and that was just commonplace. And angels, well, you could find an angel on every street corner: Joshua saw an angel and Gideon met an angel and Zechariah and Mary . . . ," we could go on and on. "Mary was probably expecting a visit from Gabriel because an angel visit was a pretty common occurrence."

Wrong, wrong, wrong! Angels were as rare back in "Bible-times" as they are today, or at least angel visits that we are conscious of. At the time when Mary lived, the Jewish people were enslaved to Rome. They were crying out for God's miracles. It's easy to imagine them saying, "Why doesn't God come and do something miraculous for us like He did for our ancestors when they were enslaved in Egypt? Where is God? Doesn't He see our struggles and our pain?" This sentiment had, in fact, been expressed in Habakkuk:

> Lord, I have heard of your fame;
>   I stand in awe of your deeds, O Lord.
> Renew them in our day,
>   in our time make them known;
>   in wrath remember mercy.
>   —Habakkuk 3:2

Habakkuk had heard what God did in the past and was asking Him to renew His miraculous deeds in his day.

So when an angel came to visit an adolescent girl, it was a shocking, incredible, extraordinary event! Gabriel was a new acquaintance, not a household name. Can you imagine how terrified Mary must have been? I'm sure the words "greatly troubled" do not do justice to the emotions she must have experienced.

Myth 2: Mary Was Not Afraid

Mary had to overcome her fear. Why else would Gabriel say to Mary, "Do not be afraid"? Mary, though, had to trust those words—and it wasn't easy to do. If a foreign presence came into your room and simply said, "Do not be afraid, you have found favor with God," would you believe that being? Sometimes I think we don't give as much credit to Mary as she deserves. Mary had to be strong in the Lord to overcome her fear and then to listen to the incredible message that Gabriel had for her.

- Here is lesson number one for us as God's chosen daughters:

Don't let fear prevent you from hearing God's incredible messages.

God has told us many times in His Word, "Do not be afraid." Do you know that "do not fear" is the command given from God more than any other command in the Bible? Do you know, precious daughter, that God is telling you, "Do not be afraid!" Instead of sending Gabriel to give you this message, He is telling you directly: "Do not be afraid precious and favored daughter."

Are you able to stand firm in the Lord and overcome your fear? Or are you paralyzed by fear like Mary could have been? What are the fears that keep you from believing with your whole heart the promises of God? Are you afraid of failing? Are you afraid of losing friends and not being popular? Are you afraid that you'll never find someone to love you? Or are you afraid of being alone? Are you afraid that you're worthless? Or are you simply afraid that you'll never measure up to the expectations you set for yourself or the expectations of others?

Whether or not we realize it, fear is something that can subtly control us and prevent us from hearing the voice of God in our lives. If, for example, we're afraid that our external appearances will never measure up to the world's harsh standards, then how can we hear God whisper to us His loving thoughts about us. How will we know how He adores us?

Recognizing fear and hearing God's voice is really a circular relationship. The more we overcome our fears and learn to believe God's Word, the more we'll hear God's voice. And the more that we listen to God's truth, the easier it is to trust Him. Conversely, the more we live in fear, the more difficult it will be to hear God's voice in our lives. And the less we hear His voice, the easier it is to be afraid.

Myth 3: It Was Easy for Mary to Believe Gabriel's Message

We might say, "If an angel came to me and told me that I was going to have a baby even though I was a virgin, of course I'd believe the angel because . . . well . . . an angel said it." Have you ever had a dream that was so vivid—seemed so real—that after you woke up, you weren't sure whether it was a dream or whether the events actually happened? I have. Sometimes, in fact, I've asked someone a question to find out if the events were real or just seemed real in my dream.

How do we know Mary didn't begin the next day and wonder, "Was it all just a dream?" I can imagine her deliberating many hours: "Did Gabriel really appear? Or am I just crazy?" It's interesting, though, that Gabriel appeared to Mary when she was all alone. You know what that means— Mary had no one to back up her story! She couldn't say to anyone, "You saw it too didn't you? You heard what Gabriel said, right?" No, *alone, Mary was forced to trust in God.* She didn't have witnesses to the miracle God had given to her. This was her message from God, and she, alone, had to believe.

It's also interesting that Mary immediately went to visit her cousin Elizabeth (Luke 1:39–40). Mary's actions speak volumes about her faith in God. I might have been wavering on the fence, wondering if what happened was really true until I had some concrete evidence (like a protruding tummy) before I believed Gabriel's message. How often we need concrete evidence to believe God. But Mary went immediately to visit Elizabeth, and Mary would have known to do this only if she believed Gabriel's message. In Luke 1:45, we read that Mary's test of her faith is rewarded: "Blessed is she who has believed that what the Lord has said to her will be accomplished!" Mary, an adolescent girl, believed God all by herself. This is truly amazing because I don't know of many things that girls do all by themselves—including going to the ladies' room!

• Here is lesson number two:

We are blessed when we believe God's Word.

Believing God isn't easy. It wasn't easy for Mary and it isn't easy for us today. Just like the laws of nature told Mary that what was supposed to happen was impossible, the laws that we see at work in the world are the opposite of God's laws.

The world says, for example, that your looks are one of the most important (if not *the* most important) factors in your life. Your appearance will determine your success, popularity, happiness, and fulfillment. God's Word says something that is the complete opposite of the world's view.

• Read and write down Proverbs 31:30.

If we really believe God's Word—that charm is deceptive and beauty is fleeting but the woman who fears the Lord is to be praised—then we wouldn't be consumed with our external appearance. Instead, we'd be consumed with fearing the Lord! We would trust that, contrary to the messages of the world, external beauty does not secure success, happiness, or fulfillment. When we allow God to take control of our external appearance and focus on fearing Him, we'll begin to receive some of the blessings He gives to those who believe. We may find that God, in fact, does a better job at making us much more beautiful than we could ever do ourselves.

• Read and write down James 4:10.

_____

_____

_____

The world says that you must love yourself, take time for yourself, promote yourself, and nurture yourself because no one else will. God's Word says just the opposite. James 4:10 says that as we humble ourselves before God, He will promote us. He will nurture us. He will lift us up.

Unless we start truly believing God and taking Him at His Word, we won't receive all the blessings that He has for us. True belief causes us to *behave differently.* If we really believe that God will honor us when we humble ourselves before Him, then we may not be as anxious when the work of others gets noticed above our own. Or we may not be as angry when we feel we've been treated unfairly. We can trust that our part is to do the humbling, and then we can leave the promoting in God's hands and be confident that He will never break His Word.

Let's go back and reflect on God's sending His messenger to Mary when she was alone. Sometimes we're so busy that we never have time alone with God and, therefore, can't hear what He is trying to tell us. At other times, though, when we're in His presence, we can hear His voice and believe His Word. But when we leave His presence we forget what to believe. We enter the world again and doubt that His truth applies there. We might search for someone else who will give our flickering belief some oxygen because we have a hard time believing anything on our own. Yet believing on our own is exactly what God desires from us. Remember that each of us lives our own story and each story is unique. Therefore, each of us alone needs to believe in the truths God gives to us.

This is not to say that we should never seek godly counsel. Mary went to visit Elizabeth. I can only imagine that Mary wanted to seek the wisdom of a woman who was further along in her pregnancy and in her belief of what God was doing in her life. God provides us with parents, counselors, friends, and pastors to support us as we seek His will for our lives. But just like Mary made a choice alone to believe or not to believe what God planned to accomplish through her, we too are faced with the same choice. Precious daughter of God, let it be said of you, "Blessed is she who has believed that what the Lord has said to her will be accomplished!"

Below is the short list of the blessings we receive as children of God. The truth we see in Luke 1:45 has been applied to each item on the list. Remember, though, that this is not a complete list!

- Blessed is she who believes she is the light of the world (Matt. 5:14).
- Blessed is she who believes she is Christ's chosen friend (John 15:15).
- Blessed is she who believes the Lord is her Shepherd and that she has everything she needs (Ps. 23:1).
- Blessed is she who believes she is chosen and appointed by Christ to bear His fruit (John 15:16).
- Blessed is she who believes she is one of God's holy people (Eph. 1:4).
- Blessed is she who believes she has an inheritance from God (Eph. 1:14).
- Blessed is she who believes she has been given every spiritual blessing (Eph. 1:3).
- Blessed is she who believes she has been created in the image of God (Gen. 1:27).
- Blessed is she who believes she is holy, and dearly loved (Col. 3:12).
- Blessed is she who believes she has incredibly great power from God (Eph. 1:19).
- Blessed is she who believes she has a wonderful future (Eph. 1:18).
- Blessed is she who believes she is precious, honored, and loved (Isa. 43:4).

Student Testimony

My high school years started off like they did for many of my friends. I had a great time in the junior high youth group and was on fire for God. Freshman year was tough with being put in a new place and a new, bigger youth group. I felt like every-one saw me as this super-happy person, and I felt that was my identity. I thought that I needed to maintain that identity no matter how I was really feeling inside. I believed that my Christianity was based on alleged "joy," which I had mistaken for outward happiness and a constant smile on my face. Because I believed that looking happy on the outside was godly, I had problems with letting anyone know how I really felt.

During my freshman year, I felt worthless coming into a big school. I felt out of place and didn't know where I fit in. I ended up finding my identity in feeling loved by a guy who was not a Christian. Unfortunately, I made many compromises and ended up feeling very separated from my friends and family. This led me right back to where I started: feeling worthless and unloved.

I started trying to hurt myself by cutting my arms because I felt this somehow relieved the pain I felt inside. I didn't feel valued or important. All through the next years I continued to carry around this lack of self worth and just covered it up with relationships with guys. If I felt they wanted me, I could pretend not to feel so bad. Of course, none of those relationships ever satisfied my deep hunger for belonging.

The summer after my sophomore year I began feeling that since I couldn't control how I felt inside, I could control how I looked on the outside. So I started becoming obsessed with my weight and how thin I could become. I loved the control it gave me over my life, which seemed so out of my control. It took a major toll on my relationship with God, but I couldn't see it at the time.

At the end of the summer I began to get attention for being so skinny, and I really enjoyed the new identity it brought me. Well, needless to say, my family figured out why I was losing the weight, and they tried to find some help for me. I went to a lady for a long day of going through spiritual warfare and refuting any lies I had bought into.

I also went to a Christian counselor who tried to work through things with me. But inevitably I wanted to hold on to the control I had over my life. So the control went from the externally obvious eating issues, to the hidden desire to end my life. I was depressed because I had all these hidden insecurities and hidden desires to feel like I truly belonged. I started fantasizing about how I could kill myself. It consumed all of my thoughts. Of course, I was still trying to keep my identity as a happy, joyful person on the outside, so that I could still feel a little valuable.

The depression became something that I could no longer hide, and after a few weak attempts at overdosing or poisoning myself, I began sharing these thoughts and feelings with my mom. This helped to let out some of the big hurts I had inside, my lack of belonging and desire to feel some identity. I went to a Christian psychiatrist for some help for the physical part of the depression and started taking some antidepressants.

While these things were okay, what I really needed was to feel my belonging in Christ and to realize how valuable I was because I am complete in Christ. I needed to see my identity in Christ. My mom had an "identity in Christ" bookmark hanging on her mirror, and that became something that I really needed to believe. Also, through the material in this study I was able to really see who I was as a child of God.

None of this was an easy process, and it was a long time before I really believed that I had an amazing identity, and it was in Christ alone. I have found that the true way to find peace and joy and happiness is to seek God and continually remind myself of who I am in Christ.

Precious daughter, God is waiting to shower you with blessings when you choose to believe Him. And remember that our beliefs are expressed through our choices. We make choices daily about whether to live by God's rules or Satan's rules. This week, will you focus on seeking God's ways and His truth? You can overcome your fear and choose to truly believe all of God's promises. Your loving Father is waiting for you. Embrace His heart for you.

| Section Two |

Believe with Your Heart

Trusting God's Truth

3

American Idol(s)

Who's on the Throne?

Our hearts are restless, until they find their rest in Thee.
                                          —St. Augustine

Have you ever felt emotionally and physically drained?

When I was in college I felt a sense of deep fatigue for the first time. I was involved in an endless number of activities, and trying to keep up with my academics and my social calendar increased my level of stress. The term "stressed out" became a frequent part of my vocabulary as well as the vocabulary of my peers.

As a wife, and mother of four small children, I now look back at that time from a different perspective. As stated in the introduction to this book, adolescence (which I consider extending through college) is an acute time of life. I see now that many of the external pressures that caused me a lot of anxiety in college were not all that significant. The pressing concerns of college, in fact, seem minimal compared to the pressures I feel in trying to grow as a godly wife and mother.

My current feelings of stress, however, do not minimize the anxiety you feel in your life right now. For most of us, the issues we struggle with during adolescence will come back to bedevil us time and again. God uses, however, whatever circumstances we're facing—right now—and the struggles we're having—right now—to lead us closer to Him. The more stress we're under, the more we're driven to cling to someone or something for help. During the stress of my adolescence I clung to some of the wrong things instead of to God. And now that I'm a mother, God continues to show me that He longs for me to cling to Him.

Today more and more of us are experiencing "stressed out" lives at an earlier age. Even junior high girls speak of being "depressed," "under a lot of pressure," or "overwhelmed." Growing up is difficult and it's normal to have some ups and downs, but when you experience high levels of anxiety and depression, that should sound an alarm. When our hearts are constantly full of worry, there's a danger that the stress in our lives may drive us to something other than God.

I'm not saying that if you're pursuing God, you'll never experience anxiety. The stressors in our lives have a purpose; they are intended to drive us to the Lord, with whom we can find peace. God may allow negative emotions into our lives for the purpose of teaching us to seek Him. Like Shadrach, Meschach, and Abednego—three Hebrew young men who were saved by God after being forced into a fiery furnace for their devotion to Him—we may meet God in a new way in the "furnace" times of our lives. If, however, we are living in a daily and consistent state of anxiety, worry, fear, or depression, we'll be "stressed out." This is a sign that something in our hearts could be out of order.

• Take a moment and ask yourself these questions: Do I often feel "stressed out"? If so, what about?

- Do I struggle with feelings of depression, anxiety, and anger? Do I often feel overwhelmed? Write down some of your thoughts.

_____

_____

_____

_____

_____

_____

During our study of chapter 1, we discussed how the world around us is under the influence of Satan. And many of us already carry too much of the world around in our hearts. Chapter 1 as well as chapter 2 of this book focused on accepting the truth versus believing the truth. Now we turn to a much more difficult subject. Who are we trusting with our hearts? When our hearts are given to the things of the world, we're destined for a "stressed out" life!

The Heart's Sway

Our hearts are very fragile. Those of us who've had a crush on someone or have been involved in a relationship in which we experienced rejection can testify to the heart's frail nature. But our hearts are not only fragile, our hearts are deceitful, and our hearts can be easily misled.

- Look up Jeremiah 17:9 and write it below.

_____

_____

_____

- Look up Proverbs 4:23 and write it below.

_____

_____

_____

Our hearts require our utmost attention. According to Jeremiah, our hearts are deceitful and wicked. All of us have the tendency to do evil. We all sway from God's laws and we turn our backs on God Himself. Proverbs 4:23 warns us that above all else, we must guard our hearts, for our hearts affect everything we do (NLT). I have to make it a priority to keep my heart devoted to God because I know from experience that my heart will be drawn to the things of this world. I experience this draw every time I go through the checkout line at the grocery store. There, my eyes scan all the magazines. The seductive headlines entice me: "Seven Secrets to the Perfect Body," or "Why Reese Witherspoon Has the Life Everyone Dreams Of."

These articles aren't necessarily evil. (Some headlines I've seen, though, I'd consider evil.) Yet as I read these articles I feel the sway in my heart—that strong pull of the world that says I should chase after the perfect body, that I should admire the life of Reese Witherspoon more than the life of Mother Teresa. I feel tempted to live for myself and pursue personal happiness as the most important goal in my life.

Yes, I'm very aware of my need to guard my heart. What's in my heart affects everything I do or, as the New International Version reads, "for [the heart] is the wellspring of life" (Prov. 4:23). I want springs of life flowing from me. I want people to come away from conversations with me feeling refreshed because they've felt God's love through me. I want to shine.

The Heart's Idols

Daughter of Christ, in order to shine you must acknowledge that your heart is deceitful and you must guard your heart. Satan is doing everything in his power to keep your heart away from total devotion to God.

Probably the most common way that Satan swings our devotion away from God is encouraging us to devote our hearts to an idol. An *idol?* Yes, it's one of Satan's oldest but most effective tricks. He knows that our hearts are designed to be devoted to something. My heart is designed for devotion and your heart is designed for devotion. The question is, *What are we devoted to?* This is how Satan deceives us: *He convinces us that we are devoted to God when actually we're serving idols.*

• Please read 2 Kings 17:27–41. What were the people who lived in Israel doing?

_____

_____

_____

_____

• In verse 35, God gives a specific command. Write it down in the following space.

_____

_____

_____

_____

Let's take some time to examine this command.

> When the LORD made a covenant with the Israelites, he commanded them: "Do not worship any other gods or bow down to them, serve them or sacrifice to them."

In this verse, God clearly commands against doing four things. The original Hebrew definitions of *worship, bow down, serve,* and *sacrifice* are below:

1. *Worship* is translated from the Hebrew word *shachah,* which is defined, "to worship, to bow down, prostrate oneself, to bow down before a superior in homage."
2. *Bow down* is translated from the Hebrew word *yareʾ,* which is defined, "to fear, revere, be afraid, to stand in awe of, be awed, to honor and respect."

3. *Serve* is translated from the Hebrew word ʿ*abad,* which is defined, "to work, to serve, to labor or work for another or to serve another by labor, to make oneself a servant."

4. *Sacrifice* is translated from the Hebrew word *zabach,* which is defined, "to sacrifice, to slaughter, to kill in religious sacrifice, to offer."

As you look at this command from God, ask yourself these questions:

• On a daily basis, what do I bow down to (emotionally or spiritually), expressing that it is superior to me?

_____

_____

_____

_____

_____

• On a daily basis, whom or what do I fear? Whom or what am I awed by and impressed with? Whom or what do I treat with honor and respect?

_____

_____

_____

_____

_____

• On a daily basis, whom or what do I serve, and for whom or what do I work diligently? For whom or what am I willing to make myself a servant?

_____

_____

_____

_____

_____

- On a daily basis, to whom or what am I willing to sacrifice and offer my time, money, and energy? Who or what in my life would cause me to sacrifice my relationships with friends and family?

_____

_____

_____

_____

Satan convinces us that we're worshiping God, yet each day we serve, bow down to, and sacrifice to our idols. We praise God on Sunday, acknowledging the facts of His Holy nature and our inadequacy, singing that life is all about Him and not about us. But come Monday, we walk into school and we're impressed by the popular girl who sits next to us in class. We may be awed by her outfit and great hair, and secretly in our hearts we've "bowed down" to her. Our awe of God has been transferred to the awe of the girl who appears to "have it all."

By lunchtime, we've served our friends by complying to their wishes, whether it be gossiping, swearing, smoking, or countless other activities. We've proven our loyal servanthood to these friends every time we in some way sacrifice God's law in order to appease them. And at the end of the day, we have little discomfort in sacrificing our relationship with our parents, whether it be through blatant disobedience or simple disrespect, because we would rather please the idol of self.

We don't have a problem, then, sacrificing those who love us if it helps us to achieve a goal. Even by Monday night, God has become an *after, after,* afterthought. We can justify all our behavior as being for good or sometimes even noble reasons. We may, for example, tell ourselves, "I couldn't confront my friends for gossiping, because it would've made them feel bad or insulted. They might think I consider myself better than them." That makes us feel a little better about not obeying God. We tell ourselves we had a good reason to do things our own way. In reality, however, the approval of our friends held more sway in our hearts than the approval of God. Therefore, the approval of our friends is an idol in our hearts. The bottom line is that we may *love* to worship God, but each day we serve, bow down to, and sacrifice to many other idols.

Everyone has different idols, but none are new to God. Whether it's intelligence, abilities, beauty, money, boyfriends, sexual pleasure, the approval of others, your body, your friends, alcohol, or drugs, God is not surprised by the things other than Him in which His children seek happiness and satisfaction. God is, in fact, so aware of this fault in our nature that He warns us about it in the second commandment.

• Read Exodus 20:2–6 and write it down in your own words.

God knows that we struggle with keeping Him first in our hearts. He addresses this in His first two commandments given to His people nearly thirty-five-hundred years ago. Many of us are aware of this famous list of God's ten commandments. Yet are we aware of how often we break commandments number one and two? I'm humbled by how often I break them. It's not easy to worship God only, and it is easy to set up idols in my heart.

A practical example will illustrate the role of present day idols in our lives. Many girls struggle with eating disorders, ranging from anorexia nervosa to overeating. During my whole life I've, in fact, known only two women who do not struggle with food issues. Every other girl and woman I've interacted with since junior high (and I'm not exaggerating) deals with battles over her body image, overeating, excessive exercise, or constant preoccupation with food and her body. Not every female, of course, has an eating disorder. Eating disorders are at the far end of the spectrum of these struggles. Yet whether we have an eating disorder or not, when we're obsessed with our bodies and food, we have a heart disorder. We are serving our idols.

If, for example, we step on the scales each morning, and if we allow the number on the scales to dictate our emotions and behaviors for the day, who are we serving? If that number is high, we may be depressed or anxious, because we haven't received the "approval of the scale." So we set out to make sure tomorrow we'll see a better number. We obsess about our weight all day, serving our "weight idol" with the majority of our mental energies. We may sacrifice supporting our friends or helping our moms because we're compelled to serve our idol through excessive exercise. Weight and body image control our lives. And on a *daily basis,* we give the best of our time, physical and emotional energies, and maybe even money to serving the idol of our perfect weight. And on Sunday, we go to church and sing about our praise and devotion to God.

• Please read and write down 2 Kings 17:41.

_____

_____

_____

_____

This verse pierces my heart every time I read it. I'm a spiritual descendent of these people. Even though the people living in the land of Israel were worshiping God, they were still serving their idols. We can worship God every Sunday and even throughout the week, but we can, at the same time, work diligently, sacrifice, and fear the idols or false gods that we've set up in our lives.

God wants our total devotion. He wants us to wake up every day and set out to serve Him, to ask Him, "How do You want me to spend my time and energy?" He wants our thoughts throughout the day to be on Him rather than on obsessions about our bodies, appearances, successes, failures, relationships, or popularity. So many of us allow ourselves to be controlled by everything else except God, so even while we faithfully worship Him, the majority of our time goes to serving our idols.

Remember that our hearts are easily deceived. It's easy to blame God for all our problems, yet we haven't been following His commands. We devote ourselves to achieving popularity, beauty, the praise of others, the perfect boyfriend, academic success, athletic achievement, or just pure selfish ambition, and then we want God to be there to solve all our problems and carry our burdens. God doesn't work that way. He loves you. *He loves you!* He knows that all of our idols will never save us, never bring us fulfillment, never protect us, or provide security. *Every idol that we serve, bow down to, and sacrifice to will always leave us drained and weary.*

If you're struggling with anorexia or bulimia, I know that you feel empty and unsatisfied. What you thought would control your negative emotions is now controlling you. You feel afraid and overwhelmed. Beloved daughter of Christ, you are precious and honored in the sight of God. Serving this idol will only leave you drained and exhausted.

And you're not alone—all of us are drained and exhausted because we've sacrificed to our false gods. Don't be afraid to give up the control and instead cling to God. Doing so may be just a beginning step toward recovery, but it's the most important step. The false god of the perfect body will never save you from the pain you feel right now, but the true, living God will not only save you, He will then set you free.

• Read Hebrews 3:12–13 and write it in the space below.

_____

_____

_____

_____

_____

When we uncover idols in our lives, we're also uncovering lies that we believe. When we turn away from the living God we do not then turn to *nothing*. We always turn from the living God to *something*. God knows our hearts—we were meant to be devoted to ONE thing. Either we will be devoted to God or we'll be devoted to something else. It's safe to say that all of us have been guilty of sinful and unbelieving hearts that have turned away from God and have bowed down to other things. The more we bow down to the idols in our lives, the more our hearts will be hardened by sin's deceitfulness.

More and more self deception means it will be easier and easier to justify what we're doing as being right. We might say, for example, "It's okay if I don't go to church, because God knows that I love him." *Wrong.* If you love God, church will not be a chore, but a blessing. "It doesn't feel wrong that I'm getting pretty intimate with my boyfriend, so I guess it must be okay." *Wrong.* Your feelings are not the guide to what is right and wrong. God's Word tells us that intimate behavior is reserved for marriage and that there are consequences for sin.

I've seen the devastation in my own life because of my willingness to serve idols. Because Satan is the great deceiver, I didn't realize for a long time how I'd lived my life for the approval of others. Although I confessed a deep love for God, I craved the approval of others and gave little weight to God's approval of me. As I was reading 2 Kings 17 one night, I was struck once again by the parents' sacrificing their children into the fire. I wondered, *How could they? How could a mother be so evil and so deceived into doing something that completely contradicts her natural instinct to love her children?*

As I was condemning these evil parents in my mind, the voice of the Holy Spirit broke through and said, "Amy, you are no better." I replied to God, "I would never do this. I would never sacrifice my children to some stupid idol." As soon as the words were out of my mouth, the truth hit me. I had sacrificed my children, my husband, my family, and my friends on the altar of winning the approval of others. I'd actually compromised what was best for my family because my main concern was what other people would think. I've been guilty of humiliating my husband and even my children because I was sacrificing to my idol. The Holy Spirit led me to write this poem through my tears:

Sacrificing Isaac

It was hard to imagine tossing babies into the fire.
What kind of mothers could be so cruel?
Were they helpless victims themselves
or willing partners in evil or both?
How is it possible to lay on the altar someone
we love so much?
I was even appalled at Abraham
for following through on God's command
to lay Isaac on a stone.
But who have I laid on the stone
that I've constructed to my false god?
My son, my daughter, my husband?
Yet unlike Abraham
I act in disobedience rather than in faith.
How deceived I have been
And how much closer to the Israelites am I.
Adrammelach and Anammelech have held altars in my heart,
and I have bowed down, served, worshiped, and sacrificed,
Oh yes, sacrificed innocent victims,
a victim myself and a willing partner in evil.
I'm no better; only my sin has a better disguise.
Disguise it no more and bring it to light.
Pour down Your mercy once again.
I will not become worthless myself,
but I will obey Your ancient Word.
Forgive me, Father, for I have sinned . . .
I have sinned.
And as with Abraham's precious son,
save those whom I have inflicted with fear and pain.
Provide for me the right sacrifice.
I will obey . . .
I will obey.

It takes a lot of courage to ask God to reveal any idols in our hearts and to let Him show us where our true devotion lies.

• Take some time to pray, reflect, and write down your response to this question: Have I sacrificed my concern for others—even of the closest relationships in my life (family and friends)—because of my service to an idol? (For example, Have you ended a relationship with a friend because she didn't make you more popular?) This is a difficult question, so take time to hear from God before you answer.

_____

_____

_____

_____

_____

If you're beginning to identify idols that you've constructed in your heart, then give praise and glory to God. Jonah 2:8 reads, "Those who cling to worthless idols forfeit the grace that could be theirs." Imagine the God of the universe coming and saying to you, "Precious daughter, here is my grace. I will lift you out of this world and I will make you free. You will not have to worry about what anyone thinks of you because you have my love. You will not have to live by Satan's rules, which lead to pain, and instead you will live by my life-giving rules. You have a special privilege. This is my grace." Then we look at God and say, "No thank you" and we cling to our idols. I don't want to be that person. I don't want to forfeit God's grace. Do you?

Regardless of whatever you're holding onto, daughter, God's grace awaits you. If you are not sensing God's peace in your life, and especially if you struggle with anxiety or depression, it may well be that you're serving an idol or idols. An idol cannot love you back. It cannot save you. It cannot help you. It only will rob you of peace and joy. Whether you cling to alcohol and drugs, a boyfriend, material possessions, food, a perfect body, academic success, athletic achievement, popularity, or even friendships, they will only rob you of peace and joy. There is only one God whom we can securely cling to and trust with all of our hearts. He is waiting for our repentance.

The Heart's Repentance

Once you've identified the idols you've constructed in your heart, how can you destroy them? Repentance is the spiritual jackhammer that will begin the destruction of our idols. To repent means literally "to change our mind and turn the other way." When we repent, we turn from the idol and toward God.

Going back, now, to my earlier illustration—the idol of the perfect body—here's a description of what this repentance might look like. When we wake up in the morning, the first thing we'll do is pray. It doesn't have to be a lengthy prayer, but instead a simple prayer of dedication like this:

> Lord, I praise You for this day. I confess that I've longed for a perfect body more than I've longed for You. I pray that You will help me keep my eyes on You today. Please whisper in my heart today Your thoughts about me. Help me to cling to You above anything else. Thank You for Your grace. I want to experience Your grace today and share Your grace with others. I love You. Amen.

Next, we hide our scales or put them in a place that's difficult to reach. This doesn't mean we will never use them again, but for right now, we need to eliminate the scales because we've used them to determine our worth. Our worth is not dependent on whether we're five, ten, fifteen, or fifty pounds under- or overweight. So we'll determine to start our day trusting in God's truth about us instead of the scale's opinion. One of my favorite passages that speaks of God's great love for me is Isaiah 43:1–4. It reads like this in the New Living Translation:

But now, O Israel, the LORD who created you says: "Do not be afraid, for I have ransomed you. I have called you by name; you are mine. When you go through deep waters and great trouble, I will be with you. When you go through rivers of difficulty, you will not drown! When you walk through the fire of oppression, you will not be burned up; the flames will not consume you. For I am the LORD, your God, the Holy One of Israel, your Savior. I gave Egypt, Ethiopia, and Seba as a ransom for your freedom. Others died that you might live. I traded their lives for yours because you are precious to me. You are honored, and I love you.

Do you want to start your day with reading a number on a scale or with reading Isaiah 43:1–4, which is taped to your mirror? God will be with you when you start feeling insecure at school. He won't let you be burned up by criticism that sometimes seems to surround you. Regardless of your weight, He paid a ransom for your freedom. He paid the price of the blood of His only Son. *You* are precious, honored, and loved.

Now instead of being obsessed with your own body, ask God to become your new obsession. After repentance, the next step is to start serving God. Ask Him as you pray what He would have you focus on that day. It may be as simple as worshiping Him. He may, for example, want you to spend fifteen minutes less at the gym and use that time to read your Bible. He will guide you as you turn your heart toward Him.

• Read and write down the first sentence of 2 Chronicles 16:9.

_____

_____

_____

_____

God isn't looking for perfection, but He is looking for fully committed hearts. This verse in 2 Chronicles is one of my all-time favorites. I've so often prayed, "Lord, when your eyes are roaming throughout the earth, please find a fully committed heart in me. I desperately want your strength, so keep my heart fully committed to You." During the postpartum period after my pregnancies (in which I gained a significant amount of weight) I said this prayer: "Lord do not *let* me lose this weight unless my heart is fully committed to you." Yes, this is a pretty scary prayer. But I didn't want to become more obsessed with shedding the baby pounds than I was with serving Him. And this is not a prayer that I could pray once and forget about. Instead, it became a regular heart cry to make sure the priorities in my life were in the right order.

God longs to bless you. He longs to hold you and give you the desires of your heart. The question is, *Will you not only worship Him, but serve Him*? Will you take the time each day to ask Him what He wants of you? Will you be awed by Him? Will you sacrifice your time, energy, and resources for Him and then stand back and watch how He multiplies everything you give Him?

You might ask "Is it possible for something I enjoy not to be an idol in my life?" The answer is *yes*. Look at the story of Eric Liddle. He was the fastest runner in his time, and he was going to race at the Olympic games. The race, however, was on Sunday, and he knew that the Sabbath was a day to be kept holy. So, even after all his work and practice, he was willing to sacrifice the race in order to obey God. God rewarded his obedience by giving him another race to run in (but a race he hadn't trained for) and the joy of receiving the gold medal.

Running was not an idol in Eric Liddle's life. He worshiped the one and only true God. The only God that can love you back is Jesus. He can save you. He can help you, and He will reward you in this life and in the one to come. He is the only God who will bring you peace and joy.

He has a great plan for you but he wants you to understand what it means to believe His truth with your whole heart. The things you enjoy in your life will not become idols when you're willing to submit everything to God. When God comes first, we find real joy in the daily activities of life.

Student Testimony

I became a Christian when I was about four years old. I was embarrassed to ask my mom to pray with me, but once she did, I sensed Jesus' presence literally all around me. I felt safe and, for the first time, sure that I was going to heaven when I died. From then on, God has been molding me and shaping me into who He has made me to be. I am still striving to reach the goal. Unfortunately, I haven't stayed exactly straight on the track at all times.

When I was in eighth grade, I was diagnosed with anorexia. So, I obeyed my parents and started to eat more. I was reluctant, stubborn, and spiritually way off course. My relationship with my parents was very tense. I was easily angered if they tried to help me. I assumed that they were judging me. I even resented both of my sisters. The oldest one, Anna, kept telling me that I was too skinny, which drove me crazy! My other sister, Cassie, was away at the time, so it was easy for me to blame her for my problems. I would tell myself I had this eating disorder because she had told me in fifth grade that I shouldn't eat so much. I went to see a counselor once a week, adding stress to my already full schedule, consisting of homework, church, friends, and cello. I was miserable.

Every morning for the past two or three years, I had been waking up, looking in the mirror, and deciding each day that I was too heavy, too fat, that so-and-so had skinnier legs or a prettier body. I would have to eat less today. I came up with all kinds of excuses. "I'm just trying to keep myself healthy by not overeating," or "I asked God to make me skinnier, so He's giving me discipline to help me accomplish that," or "I'm not starving myself. I mean, I'm eating three meals a day," or "Mom eats less than I do." These were all lies from the Evil One. I believed them all, never realizing that I was no longer focused on my God but the idol of my body.

Needless to say, it was difficult for me to worship. I thought I was doing okay. Really, I was just comparing myself to others. I would worship with the attitude that no one else was doing a good job worshiping, that I was the only sincere one, the only one right with God. There was nothing further from the truth! I was not worshiping "in spirit and in truth" like God commands. I read my Bible each morning, but I only used it for myself to point my finger at and judge everyone I knew in the youth group and at school.

I don't think that I realized how far away from God I actually was until one evening when I was going home from orchestra. I knew that a Bible study had started the week before, and I wanted to go but felt funny about walking in late. I didn't think that any of my friends would be there. But God had a different plan for me. He was faithful even though I was not. He kept tugging on my heart, making me feel very uncomfortable about going home that night and skipping the study group. I told my mom, and she turned around right away. I told her all the reasons why I shouldn't go and she said, "It's up to you, but I think that you should go." So, against my will but according to God's, I went.

There, we talked about Satan and how he is in control of this world. We talked about lies that Satan tells us. Things all of a sudden became very clear to me. I was being deceived, and I was allowing my sinful nature to drag me away and entice me, tempting me to serve more than one master. I prayed for God to free me and to reveal the truth to me. Again, my Savior was faithful!

I studied Psalm 139:14. I had memorized that verse from a cassette tape that I used to listen to when I was little. I had known it all along but had never grasped the meaning of it until that very moment. "I am fearfully and wonderfully made; your works are wonderful, I know that full well." After reading that verse, I looked up at the mirror that I had been crying in front of just a moment before—because I had seen a fat and ugly person there—and instead saw a slender (a little too slender) girl who desperately needed the Lord that the psalmist wrote about.

After that, I allowed God to work in my life. My healing was not instantaneous. It was a slow process, relearning the truth after believing these lies for so long. God was faithful to His daughter, who now humbly bows at His feet in thanksgiving for salvation and forgiveness. "My mouth will speak in praise of the LORD. Let every creature praise his holy name for ever and ever" (Ps. 145:21).

~~~

God is waiting for His children to fall in love with Him. He is waiting for them to throw away all of the worthless things that hinder them from seeing Him at work in their lives. He is waiting to free them to see His hand, provision, and love in their lives. He is waiting for *you*. Your heart will be restless until it finds its rest in Him.

4

Lies from the Dark Side

Follow the Light

> *The path of the righteous is like the first gleam of dawn,*
> *shining ever brighter till the full light of day.*
> *But the way of the wicked is like deep darkness;*
> *they do not know what makes them stumble.*
>
> —Proverbs 4:18–19

Which path are you traveling on?

The path that's full of light or the one shrouded in darkness? This may not be an easy question to answer. This chapter, though, will help plant our feet on the path of the righteous.

With chapter 3, we've just completed one of the most important chapters of our study, examining the idols that we have constructed in our hearts. Now we proceed to our next challenge—examining the lies of our hearts.

We have allowed idols to control our lives because we have believed lies. If we were not believing lies, we would not have been deceived and tricked into serving anything other than God. When we tear down idols in our hearts, we must look closer to see what the idols were made of. We'll surely discover that our idols were constructed of creative and specific lies that fooled us completely.

- Take time to read Isaiah 44:8–20. Write verses 18 and 20 in the space below, and then summarize them in your own words.

_____

_____

_____

_____

_____

_____

_____

_____

These verses should make us stop and think. The phrase "a deluded heart misleads him" is very powerful. We all have deluded hearts and are therefore dependent on God to reveal His truth to us. We must not only repent from serving, bowing down to, and sacrificing to idols, we also need to recognize and battle the lies that have filled our deluded hearts. We now have to stand up and ask, "What is this lie that I've been holding on to in my right hand?" We have to battle these lies with God's truth.

In leading small groups with this study, I find that the greatest difficulty most young women have is identifying lies of the heart. In the past, when discussing written lists of lies, groups have invariably gotten into lively discussions about what is a lie and what is not a lie. I've come to the conclusion, therefore, that all of us hold on to false ideas, believing them as truth for so long that we cannot accept that they are really lies. So this chapter is straightforward about how Satan deceives us. I make some bold statements; be prepared and willing to examine them in light of Scripture.

I believe that God's truth will always be revealed, and that if any person seeks His truth, He will not hide it from that person. If you can stick with this study, the things we'll discuss can change your life!

Lies of the Heart

This section is called "Lies of the Heart" as opposed to "Lies of the Mind" because our hearts are where the battle is waged. The mind may be where beliefs first start but they infiltrate the way we think, how we feel, and how we live.

Lies of the heart are deeply ingrained. The seeds are very small, and they are often planted in early childhood and develop into patterns of experiencing and reacting to the world around us. When we are little, we develop filters or lenses for how we view the world. If you were looking through pink glasses, for example, you'd see the world in pink. In the same way, all of us have our own set of glasses that have been created by our experiences, which—in conjunction with our minds and hearts— color our views of the world.

All of us were created to have a loving relationship with our perfect heavenly Father. But all of us are born into a sinful, fallen world where, even if we had the most loving and wonderful parents, our needs will not be perfectly met. Our parents are not God, after all, and they will disappoint us. This is reality. When the disappointment takes place, Satan will come to deceive us and plant the seed of a lie. Unless the lie is identified and uprooted, it will continue to grow in our hearts and forever color the way we experience and interact with the world. A biblical example illustrates this process.

• Read Genesis 3:1–7. According to this passage, how did the serpent influence Eve?

_____

_____

_____

• Which came first—Eve's belief in a lie or her sin?

_____

_____

In the New Living Translation, verse 6 reads, "The woman was convinced." If Eve—living in a perfect world—could be so easily convinced by Satan to disobey God, how much easier it is for us—living in a fallen world—to be deceived! Satan has not changed any of his tactics. He will use our life experiences, whatever they may be, to entice us to believe lies that go against God's Word. These lies become so deeply rooted in our hearts that we instinctively react to the people around us in accordance with the lie. We are so accustomed to believing lies, that we don't see them as something that needs to be changed. We don't, in fact, see them as lies at all. We live our lives believing lies as truth.

For me, the lie involved fear. As a little girl, I had some frightening experiences. As a result, I became fearful. When I was little, I was primarily afraid of the dark (most kids are). As I got older my rational mind convinced my heart that there was no need to be afraid of the dark, but many times my mind couldn't override my fearful heart. When I was home alone, for example, my rational mind would tell me that, in the history of my town, not one home had been broken into and the residents murdered in their beds. So the chance of that happening to me was very small. Yet my reason could not override the fear in my heart. The fear *felt* very real. It *felt* more real than actual reality.

Many years later, after dealing with fear all of my life, God showed me how Satan had deceived me. The Bible clearly states over and over again to not be afraid because God watches over His children (Ps. 91). But Satan convinced me that fear was the only thing that would protect me. My *heart* became convinced that if I was afraid of something then I would prevent bad things from happening to me. Therefore, I was afraid to not be afraid!

I actually trusted in fear more than I trusted in God. I didn't want to let go of fear because it was more comfortable to be afraid than to put my trust in God. By the grace of God, however, He showed me that He had always been my protector, and that He had always been watching over me. Fear had never been my Savior, but He has always been my Savior. Satan had deceived my heart into believing that I could control my circumstances by giving in to fear. As a result, I always struggled with obeying the command not to be afraid. *Believing a lie always occurs before we fall into sin.*

Different Means, Same End

We need to understand an important truth in discussing this chapter: *Satan will use our* different *experiences to get us to believe the* same *lies.*

Remember Melissa, Ashley, and Tracy from chapter 1? Melissa, you'll recall, comes from a very loving, Christian family and is the girl who generally has it all. She's the girl whom most of us would like to be. From the world's perspective, Melissa seems to have everything going for her. But deep inside she carries a dark secret. Melissa is depressed. She's extremely insecure and worries constantly about her life. She has even at times contemplated suicide. She wonders, *If all of my accomplishments were taken away, would I still be so well liked?* In her heart, Melissa feels that she's worthless.

Ashley, remember, from the world's perspective does *not* have it all, but she doesn't have *nothing* either. She leads a normal life. She's not the belle of the ball, but she's not a social outcast. Yet Ashley is always battling negative emotions. Her feelings about herself are as secure as a balloon that can easily be pricked. Ashley, like Melissa, struggles with feelings of worthlessness.

And last is Tracy. Tracy hides so much of her pain under her rough exterior. She may fool everyone else, but she can't fool herself. She still wishes her father would come back into her life. Even her friends, with whom she's found acceptance and belonging, do not really understand the hurt that Tracy keeps so well hidden. Tracy survives on anger. Yet in rare, quiet moments the hurt wells to the surface. Deep down, Tracy feels rejected and, like Melissa and Ashley, worthless.

These three girls have completely different life scenarios. Melissa has almost everything that the world says she needs to be happy; Ashley has no great reason for happiness and also no great reason for sadness. Tracy has seemingly none of what the world says she needs to be happy. Yet, deep inside, all of them believe the same lie: *I am worthless.* How can that be?

Satan convinces Melissa that only through her accomplishments and praise from others does she have any value. Therefore, if any of it were taken away, she would have no value. Satan convinces Ashley that, because of her lack of accomplishments and praise from others, she has no value. He convinces Tracy that because she's been rejected by her father she has no value.

Do you see how Satan works? It doesn't matter whether you possess a lot or a little, if you are loved or unloved—Satan will use your circumstances to convince you of his lies.

- Read 1 Samuel 16:7. Write this verse down in the space below.

_____

_____

_____

_____

Remember, God knows the truth about our hearts. He can see what even your closest friends or parents cannot see about you, and He wants you to know His Truth for your life. He wants you to understand what it means to believe the truth with your heart, and in believing He wants you to be healed.

During one Bible study, when I was talking about the lies of our hearts, many of the young women struggled with identifying the lies they were believing. One issue that always challenged them was whether or not it was *essential* to exercise every day. Many of the girls stated *yes*. They argued that there's nothing wrong with exercising, and it's healthy to work out daily. I didn't argue with either of these points; there is, after all, nothing wrong with daily workouts and it is healthy for you. But does God's Word say that it's *essential* to exercise every day? I then asked, "What motivates you to exercise every day?" We are motivated to action, after all, by the desires of our hearts. If our hearts believe lies, our motivations will not come from healthy desires. Take a minute to read this poem that was written by a senior in high school.

Student Testimony

Perfect

Gotta go a little faster
Gotta push a little harder
Gotta go that extra mile
Gotta be a little smarter.

Can't stop
Can't slow down
Can't break
Until I'm done
On this track I'm pressing onward
And I know I run alone.

Just keep your mind on the dream
Numbers move in one direction
The satisfaction of it all
When you'll finally reach perfection.

My muscles ache
But I can't stop
I think I almost see the top.

I can't crack
I won't give in
Gotta be the queen of discipline.

I'm almost there
I know I feel it

It's just beyond that final hurdle
But why is it that every day
Where I am is still far away?

Just ten more pounds
Then I'll be perfect
If I can get there
Then I'll smile.

Cause as you know
I find my pleasure
Every time I clear that mile.

Heads turn in my direction
Satisfied with my reflection
Body stands beyond correction
Then I'll know I've reached perfection.

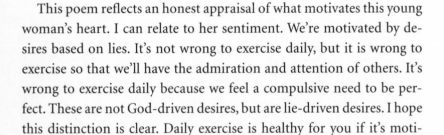

This poem reflects an honest appraisal of what motivates this young woman's heart. I can relate to her sentiment. We're motivated by desires based on lies. It's not wrong to exercise daily, but it is wrong to exercise so that we'll have the admiration and attention of others. It's wrong to exercise daily because we feel a compulsive need to be perfect. These are not God-driven desires, but are lie-driven desires. I hope this distinction is clear. Daily exercise is healthy for you if it's motivated by a pure heart.

Satan's Lies, God's Truth

Below is a list of lies, which is *not* a complete list! This list has been composed from my personal experience and from counseling girls. If you're honest with yourself, you'll probably find something on this list that resonates in you.

- Please take the time to write a prayer, asking God to reveal any lies that you are believing. He will reveal His truth to all who seek Him.

Satan's Lies

- I am worthless.
- I can't be what God expects or wants me to be.
- I have to control my life because God wouldn't control it the way I want Him to.
- I'm not beautiful.
- I have to be thin in order to be considered attractive or loveable.
- I have to be perfect.
- Being engaged with sexual activity proves that I am attractive and lovable.
- I'm a bad person and nothing can change that.
- Because of the family I come from, I will always have these problems.
- I'm the only one who struggles with these problems.
- I need to exercise every day in order to be acceptable.
- It's a sign of independence to rebel against authority.
- Other _____.

God's Truth

- God values me (Col. 3:12).
- God will complete the work He started in me (Phil. 1:6).
- God has a good plan for my future (Jer. 29:11–13).

- I am beautiful in Christ (Isa. 61:1–6).
- Beauty comes from within (1 Peter 3:4).
- God's grace is the only thing perfect within me (Eph. 2:8–9).
- Sexual activity outside of marriage only makes me feel worse about myself because it is sin (Rom. 6:19–23).
- Christ has appointed me to do His good work (Eph. 2:10).
- I am part of God's family (Eph. 1:4–5).
- Everyone struggles (Rom. 7:21–24).
- Godliness training is needed daily (1 Tim. 4:8).
- God requires submission to authority (Rom. 13:1–2).

Plenty more lies could be added to and examined on Satan's list—and don't forget that he has tailor-made for you very specific lies!

A student in one of my Bible study groups said that she'd come to realize how clever Satan really is. He will, she said, take a lie off his rack, cut it, fit it, and tailor it to suit each person's circumstances. How right she was! This was an exciting breakthrough in this girl's life. Only a year prior to that she was trapped in many of Satan's personal lies for her. But now she was not only beginning to see the truth, she was also learning to walk in the truth.

Do Your Homework

The next assignment is essential for seeing how Satan's deception can be shaping your whole life.

Take time now to complete the following "Lies and Truth" worksheets. Pray and ask God to reveal two or three lies that are affecting you, and then fill in a Lies Worksheet for each of these lies. You can make more copies of the worksheets as needed.

It's important that you fill out these worksheets and not just look at them and do them in your head. Often we can process things better when they're written in black and white, and we can see the errors in our thinking. You don't want to short-circuit this process.

After you complete the Lies Worksheets, complete the Truth Worksheets with God's corresponding truth. This is an eye-opening experience because you'll begin to see how different your life would be if, in your heart, you really believed God's truth.

Lies Worksheet 1

- The lie I have believed:

_____

_____

_____

- How has believing this lie affected me?

_____

_____

_____

_____

- How has believing this lie affected my relationship with God?

_____

_____

_____

_____

- How has believing this lie affected my relationships with others?

_____

_____

_____

_____

Truth Worksheet 1

- God's truth:

  _____

  _____

  _____

- If I believed God's truth, how would this affect me?

  _____

  _____

  _____

  _____

- If I believed God's truth, how would this affect my relationship with God?

  _____

  _____

  _____

  _____

- If I believed God's truth, how would this affect my relationships with others?

  _____

  _____

  _____

  _____

Lies Worksheet 2

- The lie I have believed:

_____

_____

_____

- How has believing this lie affected me?

_____

_____

_____

_____

- How has believing this lie affected my relationship with God?

_____

_____

_____

_____

- How has believing this lie affected my relationships with others?

_____

_____

_____

_____

Truth Worksheet 2

- God's truth:

  _____

  _____

  _____

- If I believed God's truth, how would this affect me?

  _____

  _____

  _____

  _____

- If I believed God's truth, how would this affect my relationship with God?

  _____

  _____

  _____

  _____

- If I believed God's truth, how would this affect my relationships with others?

  _____

  _____

  _____

  _____

Lies Worksheet 3

- The lie I have believed:

  _____
  _____
  _____

- How has believing this lie affected me?

  _____
  _____
  _____
  _____

- How has believing this lie affected my relationship with God?

  _____
  _____
  _____
  _____

- How has believing this lie affected my relationships with others?

  _____
  _____
  _____
  _____

Truth Worksheet 3

- God's truth:

  _____
  _____
  _____

- If I believed God's truth, how would this affect me?

  _____
  _____
  _____
  _____

- If I believed God's truth, how would this affect my relationship with God?

  _____
  _____
  _____
  _____

- If I believed God's truth, how would this affect my relationships with others?

  _____
  _____
  _____
  _____

It's helpful to review this exercise with someone who's also interested in walking in God's truth. When we share personal insights with a loyal friend, or a parent, we become more accountable. We now have someone else who knows the pitfalls we face, and often that other person can see us getting near the edge before we can see it ourselves. In this way, we can catch each other. This is a truth also found in Scripture.

• Read Ecclesiastes 4:9–12. Who do you think makes up the third strand in the triple-braided cord mentioned in verse 12?

_____

_____

_____

_____

The answer is the Holy Spirit. God will help you as you seek the truth and defeat the lies. Work with a friend so that both of you can support each other as you conquer the lies of your hearts.

Fighting the Lies

> If you do not stand firm in your faith,
> you will not stand at all.
> —Isaiah 7:9

This verse was written at a time when the King of Judah was facing an attack from two enemies. Although our circumstances are different, the truth is the same for us today. If we do not stand firm in our faith, we will not be able to stand at all.

• Read Ephesians 6:10–18. Underline in your Bible all of the words that show some kind of action. Look at the following example:

Therefore <u>put on</u> the full armor of God, so that when the day of evil comes, you may be able to <u>stand</u> your ground, and after <u>you have done everything</u>, to <u>stand</u>.

Following God's truth is not a passive process. We think that we become Christians and accept God's truth and that our part is now done. The reality is that we are in a *daily war.* Minute by minute, we need to reject Satan's lies and affirm God's truth in our lives. The first and most important step is to identify the lies we're believing. Then we need to constantly replace the lie with God's truth. If, for example, you believe you're in a hopeless situation, it's essential that you reject that thought of hopelessness as soon as it enters your mind. You can state out loud, or under your breath if you're in a crowd, "I reject the lie that my situation is hopeless, and I replace it with Your truth that You have a plan for my life, a good plan, and that I have a hope and a future."

At the beginning, you may have to state that fifty times in a day, or maybe more. You are at war, and war isn't easy. The bad news is that God's Word states that we'll be at war with the Enemy until we're in heaven or until Christ returns. The great news, however, is that we can win battles every day. It's a liberating feeling to live in victory instead of defeat!

Other action steps are essential for achieving victory in our battles: (1) flee from the lies; (2) surround yourself with truth. If you're in the habit of watching television shows and movies that indoctrinate you into Satan's lies and rules for life, then it would *greatly* benefit you to stop watching those shows and movies. If you listen to music that contradicts God's truth, it would be *extremely* beneficial to stop listening to that music. You will not fight a good war if you're surrounded by messages from the enemy. If you're feeding on a diet of lies, watching, reading, and listening to things that support these lies, you'll have a harder time digesting God's truth. Therefore, we need to do our best to flee from the sources of lies. It's impossible not to come in contact with these cultural lies, and that's why we have to be diligent about what we can control. We can reject movies, television shows, music, books, and magazines that do not reflect God's truth.

Another way to flee from lies is to take a careful look at the relationships in our lives. This is a difficult process. I'm not suggesting that we part ways with any friend or family member who is not following God. We are called to be in relationships with all types of people—Christians, non-Christians, and struggling Christians. Yet it's important that we have *close* relationships with people who are trying to walk on the path of righteousness. If, though, all of our closest relationships are with people who do not want to get out of the darkness, then we need to seek out friends who will support us as we pursue God's truth. Some natural distancing may happen in your relationships with people in darkness, and that will be difficult for your friends to understand and painful for you. But what is *most* important—your relationships with your friends, or your relationship with God?

The next action step that will help us in this war is to surround ourselves with God's truth. We need to feed on God's Word. If you're not in the habit of reading the Bible every day, now is a good time to start. The only way we'll recognize truth is if we're well acquainted with it. Taking time every day to read the Bible may seem intimidating and, believe me, I understand the feeling. My behavior isn't always consistent and I'm not an organized person. It's difficult for me to make a habit of daily activities because every day in my life is different, and I generally like it that way.

God has been gracious, though, in teaching me that He understands how He created me. I don't need to feel guilty if I am not up at 6:00 A.M., reading the Bible every day. It's more important that I have the desire and the willingness to obey. When we have that desire and willingness, God is faithful to show us how we can obey Him. He has shown me that I can read His Word throughout the day, and He gently reminds me if I've forgotten.

Many times, especially in college, I opened my Bible at 1:00 A.M. because I didn't want to lay my head on my pillow and fall asleep without reading His Word. On some days I don't have a quiet time with God (this is a risky thing for a pastor's wife to say). God always accepts us where we are. The important thing is that we turn to Him with our failures and shortcomings. He will meet us.

Another way to surround yourself with truth is worship. Worship God every day, whether that consists of listening to Christian music or simply stating, "I praise you Jesus" throughout the day. Praise will drown out the lies of Satan. When we praise God, we humble ourselves before Him and admit that He deserves our devotion. We experience more of His presence when we praise Him.

- Read James 4:6–10. Write down your favorite verse in that passage on the lines below.

  _____

  _____

  _____

  _____

- What is the promise given in verse 10?

  _____

  _____

James 4:10 is one of my favorite verses in Scripture. God promises to honor us as we humble ourselves before Him. This is a strange war we're fighting. On one hand, we need to stand like warriors and face our enemy and his lies head on. Yet, on the other hand, we need to humble ourselves like children and wait for God to honor us. As we do these things, our hearts will become indoctrinated with God's truth. I didn't realize these truths until God put me through some difficult trials.

Tough Times

As I stated previously, throughout my life I've had an ongoing battle with fear. After the birth of my first child, I became nearly paralyzed with fear. I'd been struggling with anxiety more and more since college, but having a child in my life added a whole new dimension to my fears. For some reason, one fear that always haunted me was dying of cancer. After my son was born, I started having a series of health problems. First of all I had a very difficult delivery, which my doctor said was "just about the worst delivery you could have had." This is not what a new mom wants to hear after her first baby.

When my son was three weeks old, I was in the hospital for a gallbladder attack and a bladder infection. I then suffered from one infection after another with fevers and rashes. Finally, the straw that broke the camel's back was recurring problems with dizziness. The doctor wanted to rule out a brain tumor as the cause of this problem, so he ordered an MRI.

By this time I was frantic! I was convinced that something was seriously wrong with me, and that I was going to die soon and not see my son grow up. It was a difficult time, and the fears and anxieties that I had become accustomed to living with were now consuming me. Worst of all, these health problems happened during the time of my sister's wedding—when I was supposed to be filled with joy . . . and I was filled with fear.

Praise God . . . He knew what I was struggling with, and He brought a mentor into my life at just the right time. As I confided to her what I was going through, she encouraged me to write down each specific lie I was believing and then to ask God for a specific truth in His Word that would enable me to combat each lie. As I prayed about each lie and then listened to God, He gave me verses from Scripture to combat each lie.

Most of these Scriptures were already familiar to me, but for the first time I was actively fighting Satan's lies with God's truth in a daily, minute-by-minute battle. I was standing firm in my faith and taking my "head knowledge" of God's Word and actively believing it in my heart. The result of this active faith was amazing. It was a true miracle that I was able to participate in and enjoy all the activities of my sister's wedding without the presence of fear. All of my medical problems were minor, and they were healed by God in His timing. But more importantly, I had a major victory with my spiritual problem of fear, and I can honestly say that I've been able to face fear differently since that time.

- Read Proverbs 4:18–23. How is the path of the righteous illustrated in verse 18?

_____

_____

_____

This verse is a beautiful example of what it means to seek and follow after God's truth. If you've ever seen the sunrise (which is a rare sight for me—being a night owl), you know that it is still dark as the first glow of light creeps over the horizon. Gradually, as the sun rises, the darkness recedes before the light from the sun. By noon, the sun is shining so brightly it's hard to escape its warmth. Similarly, when we begin to understand God's truth, only a faint glow of light trickles into our dark world. At that point God's truth is not illuminating our lives, but we at least can recognize it, identify it, and begin to walk in accordance with it.

As more and more we believe His truth in our hearts, and practice it minute by minute in our lives, we become filled with His light. We truly become the light of the world because now we recognize the difference between darkness and light. His truth shines brighter in our hearts, and our lives become more intense, like the warmth of the noonday sun.

The *good* news is that once you decide to reject Satan's lies and live by God's truth, it becomes easier to see His path of righteousness before you. Once you see clearly to walk this path, you won't want to stumble in the darkness again.

The *best* news is that God knows how hard it is to be in this world. He knows the trials and temptations we face today, and He knows the trials and temptations we'll face tomorrow. And although we may stumble, we will not fall. He will always be there to lead us back to the light on the path of righteousness.

Believe with Your Hands

Doing God's Truth

5

Living in Submission

Trust and Obey

Obey your leaders and submit *to their* authority. *They keep watch over you as men who must give an account. Obey them so that their work will be a joy, not a burden, for that would be of no advantage to you.*

—Hebrews 13:17–18 (emphasis added)

In seeking freedom in God's truth, we've already cleared some significant hurdles. By now, I hope that you're understanding more about what it means to believe God's truth. I hope that you're understanding His truth with your mind. Romans 12:2 says "Don't copy the behavior and customs of this world, but let God transform you into a new person by changing the way you think" (NLT). In the last two chapters, we have learned to let our minds be transformed. I also hope that you are trusting Him with all of your heart. In Jeremiah 29:13 God's Word tells us that if we seek Him with our *whole* hearts, we will find Him. It is my prayer for you that you are finding Him in this study. You've already come a long way, but our journey is not yet over.

I wish I could say that the hard stuff is behind you, but I'd be lying. Here in chapters 5 and 6 is where "the rubber meets the road." Understanding with our minds and trusting with our hearts are *essential* to our belief in His promises. But there is more to living the abundant life in Christ. If our behavior, that is the way we live out and practice God's truth, doesn't reflect our minds and our hearts, then we're missing out on the best that God has for us.

Laying Our Lives Down

Submission is a loaded word in today's culture. Our society tells us that we should submit to no one and no thing. Individuals who don't abide by the rules are glorified in movies and TV. We look at "submission" as characteristic of weakness, not strength. We have a hard time submitting to those in authority over us, especially when we don't agree with them. We can usually rationalize being disobedient or disrespectful to authority by focusing on the faults of those who are in authority over us.

This negative attitude about submission to authority has also been creeping into the church for some time. It's amazing how God's children have been deceived by Satan in the area of submission to authority. I have a personal understanding of how easy it is to be trapped into believing that you can have an obedient heart toward God, yet at the same time have a disobedient heart toward those who are in authority. I once served under a pastor for whom I didn't have a lot of respect. I disagreed with a lot of his decisions. God taught me that it was okay to disagree with this man, but it was not okay to reflect a disrespectful or disobedient spirit. I had to accept that God had put this pastor in authority over me regardless of my opinion of him. Looking back, I see that God had a purpose for putting this pastor into my life. God used that man to teach me many things I needed to learn about myself.

Satan has perpetuated this lie: *It is possible to be obedient to God and still have a rebellious spirit toward those who are in authority.* We convince ourselves that we can be obedient to God yet have a rebellious attitude toward our parents, teachers, pastors, or elders. Yet this idea is not consistent with Scripture.

· Read the following Scripture passages and paraphrase each of them in your own words.

Hebrews 5:7–9

_____

_____

Titus 3:1

_____

_____

Hebrews 13:17

_____

_____

Ephesians 6:1

_____

_____

Ephesians 5:22

_____

_____

Romans 13:1–2

_____

_____

Ephesians 5:25

_____

_____

These passages represent only a few of God's commands telling us that we need to submit to someone other than ourselves. Children need to obey their parents, wives need to submit to their husbands, husbands need to sacrifice for their wives, believers need to obey their leaders, and people need to submit to those in leadership over them.

Jesus and Submission

Look closely again, please, at Hebrews 5:7. In this passage are two very important truths about Jesus Christ that we may have overlooked.

First, *Jesus did not want to die on the cross.* Sometimes it's easy to dehumanize Jesus. We think that because He is God, He has no self-will. We assume that Jesus had no problem following the plan that God had set out for Him. Yet the Hebrews verse tells us that Jesus offered prayers and petitions with loud cries that God would save Him from death. Jesus desperately wanted God to change His mind! He wasn't excited about the suffering that He would endure.

Second, this verse tells us that because of Jesus' "reverent submission," He was heard by God. Christ, in fact, lived a life of reverent submission to God. This truth is very important. *Jesus* learned *obedience.* This is truly amazing! Jesus Christ, God Himself, Creator of the universe, Savior of our souls, *learned* obedience.

Because He came down to walk among us, Jesus learned what it meant to be obedient to His Father. Jesus had such great love for His Father and for us that he learned to be obedient to God's plan of suffering and future glory. He trusted God and obeyed Him and in doing so gave His life for the church.

Hence, Ephesians 5:25 says that husbands should love their wives as Christ loved the church. That verse really refers to an attitude of sacrifice and submission, the same attitude that Christ had as He obeyed God's call on His life.

- What are some reasons that God would establish people in authority over us?

1. To make our lives miserable.
2. To teach us the importance of obedience.
3. To make it easier to submit to an unseen God.
4. To give us a good reason to rebel.

I hope you answered 2 and 3! God knows the strength of our wills. He knows that from the time of birth, we want to do things *our own way*.

I'll Do It My Way

I have four children, and I didn't have to teach any of them to disobey me. On a regular basis, they naturally choose to do things their way instead of my way. When my daughter, Lissy, hit the "terrible twos" stage, it was with a vengeance. Once we were riding in the car and I said, "When we get home, honey, it'll be time for your nap." To this she emphatically responded, "NO NAP! NO NAP NEVER!" Believe me, the written word cannot do justice to the volume and tone in which my daughter informed me of her will.

The point is, we need practice in obedience. It's actually easier to obey the visible authority figures whom God has put in authority in our lives than it is to obey the invisible God. When we're teenagers, we often can't wait to escape from our parents' authority. Satan does a good job at tempting us with the thought that some day we won't have to answer to our parents, and we'll get to do things the way we want. Yes, it's true that you won't always be under the authority of your parents, but *you will always be under authority.*

- Take a minute to pray and ask God, "Show me if I'm struggling with a rebellious spirit." If you are, it would be helpful to write down some of the authority figures you're having a hard time respecting and obeying.

_____

_____

I Surrender

No matter what you're doing, you are called to a life of submission to God. We're all in desperate need of the Master, of His authority in our lives. Just as you live in the protection of your parents' authority, we will always live in the protection of God's authority. Don't be deceived: *We are called to a life of submission.* The sooner we understand how this truth works in our lives, the easier it will be to obey both the visible masters and the invisible Master of our lives.

To clarify a point about everything addressed so far in this chapter, the ultimate authority in our lives is God's law. Are the Nazi officers who murdered millions of innocent people justified before God because they were following the orders of their rulers? Absolutely not. God's law against taking innocent life has ultimate authority.

I can't explain why evil people become leaders—or even become parents for that matter—except for our living in a fallen and sinful world. I get sick to my stomach when I hear on the news about parents who abuse their children, or about the actions of evil rulers such as Saddam Hussein. God is in control, however, and is aware of the oppression of anyone under the authority of an evil master. No one will escape God's judgment.

Scripture refers to breaking the law of man when it is in conflict with the law of God. In Matthew 12:1–8, for example, Christ clearly states that He is the ultimate Master and that man's laws are subject to His authority. Christianity would never have spread to all people if it weren't for brave men and women willing to break Roman law and risk death for the sake of obedience to God. If, then, someone in authority asks you to do something against God's law, you are not obligated to obey that person. Remember that you serve a God of justice who sees all who are oppressed. Take comfort in the verses of Psalm 72:12–14:

> For he will deliver the needy who cry out,
>   the afflicted who have no one to help.
> He will take pity on the weak and the needy
>   and save the needy from death.

He will rescue them from oppression and violence,
  for precious is their blood in his sight.

God is aware of all of our situations, and He will not be silent. It is hard at times to trust that God really does rescue the oppressed and needy when we see so much injustice. But we have to remember that we only see this life, not the big picture of eternity. We have to trust that God knows what He is doing. I am thankful that we worship a God of justice and mercy. He will not let the guilty go unpunished, nor the oppressed unaided.

Dear child of God, you are called, first and foremost, to be in submission to God. If you are in an unjust or evil situation that involves a person in authority who is breaking a law of God, please do not be silent. Contact someone you trust to help you get out of that situation. God doesn't want us to be hurt over and over again. You may feel afraid, but take a small step of faith to get the help you need, and trust God to judge any evil master who is over you.

We can be thankful that the majority of us do not live under an evil master. Most of us, however, are under the authority of people with whom we may sometimes disagree, or toward whom we may have strong feelings of resentment. I know what it's like to be a teenager. When we are in adolescence, we direct most of our anger and resentment at our parents. These are the people who've taken care of us our whole lives, yet it is easy to have a rebellious attitude toward them. This attitude is not honoring to God.

• Reflect on the following statement and write down what you think it means:

You do not learn submission from a like-minded master.
                                                  —Gwen Shamblin

_____

_____

_____

We've been deceived into thinking that, before we submit, we need to agree with those in authority over us. Therefore, we spend a considerable amount of time arguing with our parents, teachers, and employers, trying to convince them to do what we want. If we're successful, then we'll happily follow their lead. Let's not fool ourselves, though, into thinking this is submission. Rather, it could be better termed *artful persuasion*. The word to embrace in understanding submission is *surrender*.

Surrendering requires that we give up the right to act on our opinions, and accept instead the leadership of those who are over us. When God is teaching us about obedience and submission, don't you think He will test us by having us obey leaders with whom we don't always agree? This isn't easy to do. And Jesus knows that it isn't always easy to follow God. Still, this is what He requires of us.

Blessings for the Surrendered Life

This message of submission might seem discouraging to some . . . but keep reading! Here's the good news: living a life of submission to God is the best life you could have. Remember, God *loves* you. *God loves you!* We can never imagine how much God loves us and loves to shower His blessings on us.

I love to give gifts to my children. I, in fact, spend far more money on them than I do on myself. I love to shower them with treats, presents, special surprises, and fun activities. It gives me great joy. Most of the time, I shower them with surprises and presents (especially at Christmas and their birthdays) just because they're mine. My husband and I always want them to know that they are loved and accepted by us. Our love is not contingent on how smart they are, or how attractive they look, or how well they behave. We, in fact, make a practice in our home of having a conversation with each of them that goes like this:

"Lissy, I love you very much. Do you know why I love you?"
"Because I'm good?"

"No, you're good, but that's not why I love you."

"Because I'm a good artist?"

"No, you're a great artist, but that's not why I love you."

"Why do you love me?"

"Because God gave you to me. How did I get to be so lucky to be your mommy? God must have thought I was pretty special because He picked me to be your mom."

This is truly how my husband and I feel about our children. We often wonder, "How did we get to be so blessed to have such wonderful children?"

We communicate to our children that we love them no matter what. But we also communicate to them that when they're disobedient, we have to hold back things we would desire to give them. When, for example, my children complete their chores for the week with good attitudes they're rewarded with either a small amount of money or maybe a special surprise. Yet when my kids are disobedient, they don't receive these rewards, and sometimes we have to take away a favorite toy. I never *enjoy* doing this. As a parent, I want my children to have special treats and do fun activities, but I have to give them less than I desire in order to teach them the importance of obedience.

Why do my children need to obey me? Because my husband and I love them, and want what's best for them. My son JD loves sugar! If he had his way he would have a steady diet of candy, cookies, and ice cream. My husband and I do our best to moderate his addiction. Yet JD is not happy with us when we say no to dessert or extra treats. And if he throws a tantrum because he didn't get what he wanted then he has to go in time-out, and he really does not like that. Disciplining JD is not much fun for him, or us, but it would not be good for JD to live on a sugar-only diet. We discipline him because we love him. We want what is best for him.

It's the same with God. God loves to give us what we want. God loves to bless us. God longs to lavish us with His love in ways that we cannot even dream of. He will never, though, give us something that's not good for us—even if we really want it! He is our loving Father who wants to bring joy into our lives. But when we're disobedient—which means doing what we want instead of what God wants—He cannot bless us in the same way He would if we were walking in obedience. He may even have to take away things that we like if it will help us to turn to Him. God does this because He needs to teach us to obey Him, and because He knows what's best for us.

Of course, not all the negative things that happen to us are due to our disobedience. Look at the life of Job. He walked in obedience before the Lord, yet he suffered many hardships that God allowed into His life. We learn things about God in the trials of our lives that we'd never learn if everything was smooth sailing. So obedience is not the ticket to an easy life with no troubles. Yet disobedience will lead us into more trouble and deprive us of some heavenly blessings that we don't want to miss.

Just like any earthly parent, God wants the obedience of His children. And like any earthly parent, God longs for our love. Every time my children tell me that they love me, I'm filled with joy. Many of us find it easy to tell God of our love for Him. We, in fact, sing about it every Sunday morning. One of my favorite worship songs is "I love you Lord." I can sing this song to God with great passion. And God is enraptured by my love because He loves to hear His children express their hearts to Him. Yet I've been convicted that my life doesn't always *reflect* my love for God.

- Read John 14:15, 21, 23–24 and John 15:9–11. What point do all of these verses emphasize?

  _____

  _____

  _____

God has made it clear in Scripture that we show Him our love by *obeying* Him. Just like I'm proud of my children when they obey me, I want God to be proud of me. I want to hear the words, "Well done, good and faithful servant." I can just imagine God on His throne, looking down on me with a proud-daddy grin every time I follow His will. I can hear Him say to the angels, "That's my girl." Even as I write these words, tears fill my eyes because I can also see the look of disappointment on His face for every time I've failed. I can hear Him say to me, just as I do to my children, "It's not that I don't love you Amy, it's just that I'm disappointed when you don't obey me. I love you and I want to bless you, and I'm sad when I have to withhold anything from you because of your disobedience."

Obeying God requires that He is number one in our hearts. It's easy for us to be upset with God when things aren't going the way we want them to go. But maybe we need to stop and look at ourselves and see how we're doing at obeying God. Do we say *no* to the things we want and *yes* to what God wants? We have to be willing to examine our hearts and ask God if we are being disobedient in any area of our lives. God desires us to obey His Word, and He wants our moment-by-moment obedience as we listen to His voice in our hearts.

We live in a culture, though, that has almost completely forgotten the idea of obedience. I know that I had almost forgotten. I admit that until recent years, I had deceived myself into believing that I was obeying God, when all the while I was obeying my will instead. During my senior year in college, for example, I got engaged. I was involved in a relationship with a Christian young man whom I thought I would marry. While we were dating, however, I was actually drifting further from my relationship with God.

Right after my boyfriend proposed and I had the ring on my finger, I heard an inner voice warning me that this was not right! I quickly dismissed, though, the thought that what I was doing could be wrong. After all, I was engaged to a Christian man, from a Christian family, and we were in love. What could be wrong? As the relationship began to fall apart, it became clearer to me that I couldn't make things work. I began to surrender to God my desire to marry this man. Over and over again I would pray to God, "Lord, I don't want this if you don't want it for me, even if it hurts to give it up." Eventually, I did end the engagement, although it was painful because I didn't want to.

God used this experience to teach me that His will and my will won't always be the same. Would I be willing to obey Him? In the end, my choice to obey proved that, once again, God's will is always the best way. My husband, Rob, is the greatest blessing in my life. I cannot imagine being married to anyone else. God's will is not just the best way, it is the only way.

I recently heard in a Bible study, "There's no comfortable alternative to God's will." We may not want to do things God's way but we'll be lost doing it our way. We may not want to obey our parents, but we won't find the freedom we're looking for in disobeying our parents. You may find a temporary kind of freedom, but negative consequences always occur when we follow our own paths.

- Read Deuteronomy 30:11–20. In verse 19, God gives His people a choice between _____ and _____, and _____ and _____. When we disobey God, what, according to this passage, are we choosing?

  _____

  _____

We won't, of course, be struck by lightning if we disobey God. If that were the case, no one would be left on the planet. This passage refers to a general pattern of life and blessings as we seek to obey God's will, versus a pattern of curses and spiritual death as we do things our own way. No one can obey God perfectly—that's why we all need a Savior. We do not *save* ourselves when we obey God, yet our obedience *demonstrates* our love to Him.

Please don't be discouraged if you're struggling to obey God. If you're struggling, you're right where He wants you to be. It's not easy to do things God's way. It's not easy to honor our parents when we're feeling hurt by them. It's not easy to end a relationship with a boyfriend because it's causing us to sin sexually. We will struggle with obedience our whole lives, but the more we choose to obey, the less we will struggle. And when we mess up, God is waiting for us to run to Him. He desires to fix everything that's broken in our lives and heal us, even when we make mistakes.

He also desires obedient children. Are we willing to stop being disobedient children and commit ourselves to obey Him? A girl in one of my small groups said, "I kept praying to God to pick up all the pieces of my life and put them back together again. Then," she said, "I finally realized that I was still holding some of the pieces." It's a very difficult thing to die to our own wills and truly to let God carry all the pieces of our lives.

Please take a look at one more verse as we conclude this chapter on submission and obedience.

• Read Matthew 10:39 and write it in the space below.

_____

_____

_____

It's easy to think, *This verse is for martyrs and missionaries, not for me.* I used to believe that. But God gave this command to everyone, not just those who were heading out to the mission field. God wants to give to you an abundant life. The only way He can do so is if we let go of control and submit to Him in all areas of our lives.

This means not only avoiding sin in our lives, but also obeying His Word and listening to His voice. It means sitting next to the girl at lunch who's all alone, and dying to your own desire to be with your friends, because you know this is what the Holy Spirit is prodding you to do. It means sacrificing money that you want to spend on yourself because you feel God telling you to give it to the church for His purposes. There's no question—this is hard stuff to do. But believe me, *our God in heaven will bless you in ways that you cannot imagine when you begin to daily die to yourself and live for Him.*

An old hymn has a chorus that would be a great theme song for our lives:

> Trust and obey
> For there's *no* other way
> To be happy in Jesus
> But to trust and obey.

The line, *"There's no other way to be happy in Jesus,"* is very convicting. If we could only remember this each day, we would unleash God's power in our lives for abundant living!

As stated before, there's no comfortable alternative to God's will. We might think, *What if God's will for me isn't what I want?* God knows what's best. Do you trust Him?

We also think, *If I do it my way and get what I want, then I'll be happy.* We even compare our lot with others, seeing other people get what we want and deciding what they have will make us happy. Thinking this way is dangerous! You'll never walk in another person's shoes, and you don't know how happy and content that person is . . . or isn't.

Our concern is not just for this life, but also the life to come. I urge you, beloved daughters of the King, trust and obey God's plan for *your* life. He won't let you down.

Loving by Doing

The JOY of the Lord

A person completely wrapped up in himself makes a small package.

—Harry Fosdick

We now approach the end of the Shine study.

I hope that you've grown in understanding and that you are embracing God's heart for you. I hope you are eager to live for Him.

In this last section, we've been learning what it means to believe God with our hands, to live out His truth in our daily lives. The evidence that God's truth is shedding light in our minds and hearts is in the outpouring of His Spirit in our *behavior*. And our behavior is the part of our Christian walk that is most visible to those around us.

This study came out of the leading of the Holy Spirit to help young women live the truth of who they are in Christ. Let's take a minute and revisit the theme passage in 2 Timothy.

• Read 2 Timothy 3:1–7. Underline in your Bible the words in these verses that are related to "love." Then write verse 7 in the following blank.

_____

_____

_____

There isn't enough time in this study to answer the question of whether we're living in the last days. We *may* be approaching the end times and, if so, we can waste no precious days, hours, or minutes in doing the will of God. In 2 Timothy 3:1–5, you'll notice the "misuse" of love that is evidenced in these terrible times. Here, Paul (the author of 2 Timothy) refers to people being "lovers of themselves," "lovers of money," "without love," "not lovers of the good," "lovers of pleasure rather than lovers of God." Apparently, the world we live in is characterized by a lack of love and the abuse or misuse of love.

We want to be women who are the complete opposite of those Paul describes in 2 Timothy 3:6–7. Instead of being weak-willed, we want to be strong-willed—but strong-willed for the Lord.

Have you ever been told that you are strong-willed? Often the term *strong-willed* carries a negative connotation. But in this case, our strong wills are in submission to God's authority. It takes a strong-willed woman to practice God's truth in our world. It takes a strong-willed woman to reject the lies of Satan and trust Christ for her identity. It takes a strong-willed woman to bring love to a world that's desperate for it. So if you've ever been labeled "strong-willed," take heart and embrace what God has given you. We all need to become strong-willed daughters of Christ who are willing to stand up for truth in a dark world.

We need to be clear, though, about why we are fighting. What is our purpose? We evaluate our walk with Christ on many different levels. We gauge our spiritual growth on how faithful we are at doing our devotions or the state of our prayer lives. We may evaluate our spiritual lives by our faith in God, how we feel about ourselves, or our struggles with sin. None of these evaluation methods are wrong, but they may keep us from evaluating our ultimate purpose for being in this world.

- Read Mark 12:28–34. What did Jesus say is our purpose in this life?

  _____

  _____

  _____

- Why do you think Jesus told the teacher of the law that He was *not far* from the kingdom of God?

  _____

  _____

  _____

That second question is difficult to answer. In the past, I believed that Jesus told the man that he was "not far" from the kingdom of God because he was standing near Jesus—a simple matter of proximity like the game of Hot and Cold. If you're closer to Jesus you're closer—warmer . . . warmer . . . hot, hot . . . very hot—to the kingdom of God. This probably isn't the most theological explanation of Christ's response to the man.

A better question would be, *Why didn't Jesus answer the man, "You got it; that's the answer, that's it!"* Then Jesus would praise him for getting 100 percent on his pop quiz. The man did, after all, respond with the right answer. Throughout the Bible, God wants one thing from His children—their love. And He wants to see His love become more abundant in the world.

Perhaps Jesus told the man that he was "not far" from the kingdom of God because Jesus knew understanding and action are two different things. The man *knew* the right answers, but how was he *doing* at loving God with all his heart, soul, mind, and strength, and how was he doing at loving his neighbor as himself? Giving lip service to God's commands and following God's commands are not the same thing. As already seen in this study, believing God's truth begins with understanding His truth in our minds, trusting Him with our hearts, and serving Him with our hands.

From this passage in Mark, we derive the one all-important evaluation tool for determining how we are growing spiritually. We each need to ask, *How am I loving?* How well am I doing at loving God? Am I obeying Him in the big and little areas of my life? How am I doing at loving my parents? Do I obey, honor, and respect them? Do I forgive easily, or do I often carry a grudge? Would my friends describe me as a loving person? Do I show love to my enemies? What am I doing to express my love for the lost and for Christians who have offended me?

These are convicting questions. Even as I write them I'm convicted about my own lack of love. It's not easy to forgive when we've been wronged. I have a hard time loving my enemies. I need to ask myself the questions above—and to keep asking them. We can be faithful at doing our devotions, attending church, avoiding sin, but if our lives are absent of love, what have we gained? This is exactly what Paul was referring to in 1 Corinthians 13.

- Read 1 Corinthians 13. Use the space provided to practice the following exercise.

  Directions: Pray and ask God for a list of people whom He wants you to "insert" into this passage. Take the time and write down verses 4–7, using each person's name, and reflect on how well your behavior has measured up to this test of love. This is a hard thing to do and very valuable.

- When it comes to my parents, I am patient, I am kind . . .

- When it comes to my friend _____, I am patient, I am kind . . .

_____

_____

_____

_____

- Write down your own paraphrase of 1 Corinthians 13:1–3.

These verses tell us that our gifts, our knowledge, and even our service amounts to nothing if we don't have love. The kingdom of God, you see, is *love*. That sounds almost fairytale-ish, but it's true. Why did God send Jesus to the world? Because of *love*. The whole message of the Bible is really about love. The Bible tells us that *God is love*. Think about this for a minute: how would we know what love is without God? The whole purpose of the existence of humanity is to demonstrate *love*. In Romans 5:8, we read, "While we were still sinners, Christ died for us." God sacrificed His own son for a people who completely rejected Him. How would we ever know what *love* truly meant if it were not demonstrated for us?

As children of God, then, we need to remember that we are called to continually demonstrate His love in this fallen world. We need to demonstrate, teach, model, and exemplify a love that is supernatural. Our behavior needs to stand out in a world that's starving to know the true meaning of love.

Overcoming the Obstacles

- What do you believe is the number one thing that prevents us from loving others as God has called us to do?

One way to answer this question is to look at the divorce rate in our country today. When people get married, they take vows to love and cherish each other "'till death do us part." As we're well aware, many couples don't follow through on their vows. In my experience as a marriage counselor, the reason people often give for not staying married is that they don't feel in love anymore.

Another of Satan's most successful and destructive lies in our culture is that we should judge everything by our feelings. The theme song of a children's TV show has a line that makes me cringe: "If you learn to trust your feelings you can never go wrong." I don't know about you, but to me that line is sheer craziness. I'm not always an emotionally stable person (my husband would back me up on this), and I can't imagine all the trouble I'd be in if I "trusted" my feelings. In my own experience, living according to my feelings has often led me into problems rather than navigating me out of them.

You may not know what it's like to be married, but most of us are well-acquainted with a married couple (probably our parents). Trusting my feelings doesn't always have the best result in my marriage. At times my husband does or says things that make me feel like he doesn't love me. When I act on this feeling, I end up hurting him by something I say or do. In reality, the vast majority of my husband's words and actions communicate over and over to me that he really loves me. Yet it's easy to forget all that when I'm feeling hurt. I have a tendency (we all do) to act in accordance with the hurt feeling, not with reality.

I'm not saying that emotions are irrelevant and should be ignored. God gave us our emotions, and emotions are good indicators of the states of our hearts. If, for example, we find ourselves angry a lot, that means that we need to examine what's going on in our hearts that's producing so much anger. Usually we'll find that we've been hurt, and we have to deal with our hurt so we can resolve our anger. What we do not want is to let our anger guide our decisions and behaviors. That's why "trusting" our feelings can get us into a lot of trouble. Emotions are very important but they're not a benchmark for guiding us through life.

The diagrams below may help illustrate the different role that feelings have taken in our culture. Many years ago, a gospel tract used a diagram of a train to demonstrate the role emotions should have in our lives. The tract explained that a healthy spiritual life consisted in knowing the *facts* about God, having *faith* in God, and then your *feelings* would eventually fall into place.

In this model, feelings were looked at as the tag-along caboose that didn't need much attention.

In response to the idea that emotions are basically irrelevant to our spiritual life, another trend started creeping into the church. As the secular world started paying more and more attention to feelings in regard to personal health, Christians also recognized that God created emotions and that they're important to our well-being. In our culture, however, feelings have become the driving force behind our decisions and behaviors. The little train on the track might, in fact, look like this if we drew it as a picture of today's culture.

This shift in the importance of feelings has been so subtle that we don't realize the impact it has on us. Some examples of this impact are illustrated by how we view loving God and loving ourselves.

Loving God

I don't know how many times I've said this or heard other young people say it: "I don't feel close to God right now." As a result of this lack of "feeling close to God," we often find ourselves struggling spiritually. As a youth-pastor's wife, I've taken many mission trips, and I can tell you that God does something amazing in our lives when we take the time to serve Him. These trips are often emotional "highs" or described as "mountaintop experiences."

During these trips, students often report feeling so close to God and seeing His power in a more vivid way. Yet when students get back from these trips, they feel a spiritual dryness. They think something is wrong in their relationship with God because they're not *feeling* the same way. As a result, they may stop spending time in God's Word, stop attending church, and fall into disobedience. It's easy at this point to blame God for the lack of closeness, but in reality *we* have stopped spending time with Him. *He* has never changed.

• Read and write down Hebrews 13:8.

God never changes; your emotions change! Our lack of warm, fuzzy feelings toward God often causes us to stop putting Him first in our lives, yet if we *love* God we will persist in obeying Him even when our feelings are not what we'd like them to be. This is the nature of love. Love persists even when feelings have stopped.

A way to overcome this obstacle in loving God is always to acknowledge *all of your feelings* to Him. God does care about your emotions. He has seen every tear you've cried from the day you were born. He wants to hear about your sadness, your anger, your disappointment, your fears, your joys, and your desires. Any loving father is interested in what his children are feeling.

As a parent, I consider it a treasure when my children are able to share their emotions with me. The other day, my son RW was obviously upset but he didn't want to talk about what was bothering him. Throughout the day he kept his negative feelings inside. As a result, he had trouble getting along with his siblings and was generally irritable. When he was about to go to bed, he finally opened up and shared with me what was bothering him. As his mom, I not only had compassion on him, I was also so thankful that he would share his feelings with me.

It's not easy to share our negative emotions with others, especially our parents. But good parents want to know what their children are feeling. And since our heavenly Father is perfect, how much more does He desire for His children to share all of their emotions with Him. Therefore, let your emotions, positive and negative, drive you to God. Let the *constant truth* of His love for you be the driving force behind your love for Him.

Loving Ourselves

The following is a bold statement: we all love ourselves. Yes, *all people love themselves.*

- Please read Mark 12:31 and write it down.

_____

_____

_____

- If we didn't love ourselves, how could God command us to love our neighbor as we love ourselves?

_____

_____

_____

The power of Satan's deception never ceases to amaze me and convince me of my absolute need of Christ. For a long time I struggled with a low self-esteem. People who have a low self-esteem have trouble loving and accepting themselves. I'd been deceived into thinking that I needed to spend more energy learning how to love myself. No one has to *learn* how to love herself or himself; it's natural from birth. If not, the command from God in Mark 12:31 would make no sense. No, the reason God can give this command is because He knows that loving ourselves is *natural* and loving others is *unnatural.* Therefore, He commands us to *learn* to love others as we naturally love ourselves.

Some common questions come to mind in response to the preceding paragraph. If I naturally love myself, then why do I have so many negative feelings about myself? Or if all people love themselves then why do some people commit suicide? The answers lie again in misunderstanding the concept of love. We're so brainwashed into believing that love is all about feelings. Therefore, when we have negative feelings about ourselves we mistake this for not loving ourselves.

Negative feelings about ourselves are very powerful and can lead people to do something as drastic as trying to take their own lives. Negative emotions can result in us not taking care of ourselves. Or we may lash out at others because we feel badly about ourselves. But these negative feelings are often the result of self-protection. We're born with the drive to protect ourselves from the world. This self-protection is self-love. Even when we have a low self-esteem, we tend to have a preoccupation with ourselves, not a lack of self-focus.

One of the saddest things I've witnessed in my ten years of youth ministry is when precious and honored young women spiral downward because of feelings of insecurity. I'm saddened because I see these girls cover up these negative feelings by making choices that actually hurt themselves. Whether drinking, smoking, engaging in sexual activity, cutting, or other self-destructive behaviors, these precious daughters of God are driven by their negative feelings about themselves instead of God's feelings about them. All of these behaviors offer these young women temporary self-comfort.

Even when we do things that hurt ourselves, our actions reveal that we do indeed have no problem with self-love. Especially when we're hurting, we feel the need to protect ourselves, save ourselves, rescue ourselves from our pain, and focus on our own needs. Are not all these the actions of love?

Guess what? God loves you. He wants to protect you and save you. He wants to rescue you from your pain and attend to your needs. He can lead you on a path where you'll experience His feelings about you. And His feelings can become your feelings!

Remember at the beginning of this study, it was stated that Satan's job is to distort God's truth. God's truth is that we need to have our focus on loving Him and loving others. Our emotions, then, lead us down the path of self-love and self-focus. And we are so deceived by our own emotions that we think the answer to our problems lies in deeper and deeper self-focus. But when we view our negative emotions not as truth but as warning indicators, those emotions lead us to God. Feelings of worthlessness, for example, do not mean "I am worthless." Those feelings should instead lead us to pray, "God, I know I'm not worthless. Show me why I'm feeling this way."

God doesn't want you to have negative feelings about yourself. *Let God, instead of your emotions, guide you.* He has the power to bring us to a place where we're free from paralyzing self-centeredness. As we begin to love Him first, His love in us enables us then to love others. We then experience His love for us in fresh, new ways.

Love and Light

There is a line in an old praise chorus that reads, *"they'll know we are Christians by our love."* How true this is! The world is desperate for the children of God to walk in the love and the light of His *truth.*

- Read 1 John 2:10–11.

> Whoever loves his brother lives in the light, and there is nothing in him to make him stumble. But whoever hates his brother is in the darkness and walks around in the darkness; he does not know where he is going, because the darkness has blinded him.

Love and light are often connected in Scripture. We serve the God of light and we serve the God of love. We cannot love others or God in our own power, but through Jesus living in us, we can. In the above passage from 1 John, God is telling us that living a life that practices His love is also living in the light.

I stumble. I stumble loving my friends; I'm not always there for them like I want to be. And I stumble loving my enemies; it's hard for me to love people who are mean to me. Yet when I see that I'm stumbling and I'm honest with myself, I know the real reason I have trouble loving others is because of the darkness in me, not the people around me whom I'm so quick to blame. The more that I experience God's great love and forgiveness for me, the more I feel capable of loving those around me. God is calling you, precious daughter, to step out of the darkness and to practice His love. *Love* Him, love others. *Love, love, love.*

So many things we learn in childhood are truly the secrets of life. They are very simple truths. God tells us that we need to know Him with a childlike faith because children so naturally accept God's truth. My mom has taught first-grade Sunday school for twenty-five years, and every Christmas she has her class make the same banner. This is how the banner appears:

Jesus
Others
You

There it is. A very simple message that even a young child can understand. The way to have *joy* in your life is to put Jesus first, others second, and yourself last. I pray that I can live out this simple truth in my life. I pray that you can live this out in your life. And I pray that the *joy* of the Lord would become the truth that defines us.

Conclusion
He Is Enough

As you complete this study I hope that you've been challenged, encouraged, and inspired by the Holy Spirit. More important, I pray that you have come to experience God's love in a deeper and more meaningful way. His love is the only thing that will never let you down. The love of our heavenly Father is the only permanent fixture in our lives.

This study is only the tip of the iceberg, only the beginning of a journey to becoming a godly woman in today's world. God is waiting for His children to be devoted to Him. He is waiting to show us that He alone is enough in our lives.

Are you ready to believe God with your head, heart, and hands? The world is waiting for young women like you to live according to God's truth. You will shine like a star in a dark and depraved world. If your goal is to blend in with the world around you, then this study has probably been a waste of your time. But if your goal is to shine, then I hope there is already a glow on your face.

When my one-year-old daughter Marlayna was born, I had a wonderful godly doctor who performed the delivery. He gave her to me so I could hold her, then he took her over to the baby table for a thorough examination. As he was checking her so tenderly, he spoke a blessing to her: "Marlayna, you are a special creation from God. There has never been anyone like you and there will never be anyone like you again." I can barely write these words without crying! What an incredible blessing to be spoken over you as you come into the world.

What my doctor said is true. There has never been and there will never be another Marlayna Angenette Rienow. And there has never been and will never be another *you!* I speak the same blessing to you now. You are a special creation from God. God has a plan that is intended for you. He wants you to start believing Him now. He longs for you to abandon any idols in your life that are preventing you from total devotion to Him. Give Him your whole heart. Trust God to guide you, save you, and protect you. And bring to Him all your feelings. As you read God's Word, you will learn more and more about His feelings for you.

The best way to conclude this study is to share one more example of the Holy Spirit's power in the life of one of His children.

Daddy's Girl

It was a very cold day when the doctor presented this little one to her father. "It's a girl," the doctor said. The father said under his breath, "I know." He thought how he had always known that "it" was a girl. This little baby girl was his beloved. He remembered the day that she was conceived, and he knew all along that she was going to be a special light in his heart.

She grew up exactly as he'd expected. She was bright and full of life, smart, funny, and a joy to be around. She quickly captured the hearts of others because of the happiness that seemed to radiate from within her. And although her dad enjoyed all of these things, this is not what delighted him about her. His delight came from the joy he had every time she ran into his arms, and whispered into his ear, "I love you, Daddy." This was his delight.

Whenever she came to him, he would say to himself, "This makes it all worthwhile. Her love is worth having to deal with the messes she makes, the temper tantrums, the times she is disobedient, rude, or disrespectful. All the hard work it takes to see a daughter grow up is worth it in order to have her love. It's worth everything I have."

Likewise, to this little girl, her father was the most special person in her world. She had a perfect sense of peace just knowing her daddy was there. Sometimes, she'd fall asleep in his arms and just rest in the presence of his love. Sometimes she'd spend the day doing her chores and playing with her friends and have little time to see her daddy. But it would not affect her love for him. Whether she was with him or not, she was assured of his love for her.

And, of course, she loved being with him. They would spend time together, whether camping, on bike rides, or on trips to the ice cream parlor. He would let her know how special she was, and she carried this with her. Every time her daddy wrapped his arms around her, she would think, *All I really need is you.*

As she grew up, her relationship with her dad very slowly changed. Although they were still close, she began to think that she needed a lot more than he could give her. Nor did it take her long to see that just because her dad loved her didn't mean everyone else did.

She had her basic childhood struggles, no more or less than any other kid. She had good friends and also had the type of friends who betray you and stab you in the back. Likewise, she was a good friend to some and she betrayed others. She was liked by some kids and teased by others, just as she liked some kids and teased others. She was a good student, but not the best student. She was attractive, but not a stunning beauty. She had once thought she was a respectable athlete, but being picked last to be on a soccer team convinced her otherwise.

And through all these struggles, her dad would let her know that he loved her, that he thought she was special. And even though she knew it was true, she thought, *So what?* In her eyes, her dad couldn't make *everyone* like her, or the mean kids go away, or make her a better soccer player. Her dad was no longer enough to make her happy.

As she grew up, she worked hard to be liked by everyone. She, in fact, had it down almost to a science—how to win the approval of others. She could mold herself any way she needed to receive favorable opinions from others. She became an expert at reading other people's reactions to her—at least she thought she was an expert. If she thought someone didn't like who she was, she'd simply modify herself in order to fit that person's expectations. She would often walk away from a conversation with another person wondering whether she'd failed or succeeded in winning that person's approval.

She developed different skills that were admired by others and sacrificed other skills that didn't win as much admiration. And in all these efforts, she became very successful. She accomplished much and won the admiration of many.

Her dad, though, watched his precious little girl become whom everyone else thought she should be instead of the person he knew she really was. He felt like he'd planted a seed and waited for a beautiful flower to grow, but watched weeds choke the flower so it could never bloom. The flower sometimes would almost bloom, but then a weed would creep around it and choke it.

Although it saddened him to no longer see her smile, hear her laugh, and have her complete love, it broke his heart to see his little girl foolishly waste her time and energy on things that he knew would ultimately be meaningless. It seemed that she never had the time to run to his arms and whisper, "I love you." They didn't spend time together, doing the things they enjoyed. It seemed that she, in fact, no longer loved him, but loved only what he could do for her.

He was happy, of course, even if she came to him only when she was in trouble. Sometimes, though, he practiced tough love. Although it made his heart ache to watch her suffer the consequences of her own behavior, he was ultimately upset because she disregarded everything he'd taught her and attempted to do things her own way.

He wanted to be that daddy again who could gently guide her and she would listen. He wanted to be the strong father who could help her up and dry the tears when she skinned her knee. He wanted that look in her eyes that said, "I know everything is all right when you are here." He just wanted to take care of her, but she wanted to take care of herself.

When she became a young woman, she was still as insecure as a little girl but maintained a false appearance of strength. In the eyes of everyone around her, she was successful, but in the eyes of her father she had traded his love for the love of others. She had sacrificed what he wanted her to be upon the altar of what others wanted her to be. But he never forsook her. Even when her own sin got her into trouble, he was always there waiting with open arms. He longed to have her come back, rush into his arms again, and whisper, "I love you, Daddy."

As the years went by the young woman became more and more stressed, more and more anxious, more and more negative. Most of all, she became more and more tired—tired of working so hard to please others, tired of living up to standards that she could never keep, tired of struggling with the same feelings she had when she was ten. She was tired of feeling not good enough, smart enough, pretty enough, talented enough. . . . You name it, it was never enough.

And now it was not just her, but her husband whom she

saw as not smart enough, or handsome enough, or kind enough, or sensitive enough. Her friends were not enough. Her family was not enough. *Nothing was enough. Nothing could bring contentment and nothing could bring peace.* She always needed something more—something she should be doing or something she should be changing about herself. She wondered if this was what life was about—being trapped in an endless cycle of trying to accomplish more and win the approval of others—because this was overwhelming and tiring.

Then one day she thought she heard a voice saying, "Remember when I was enough?" *Remember when I was enough.* . . . The voice became clearer now. "Remember when you said, 'All I really need is you'? You see, Amy, I have loved you from the time I first conceived of you. I have adored you since before you were born.

"I have felt the pain of watching you love so many things besides me, all the time knowing that you would never be content until you turned to me, until you let me wrap you in my arms, and until you once again whispered in my ear, 'I love you, Daddy.'

"This is what I long for from you. Not your talents, not your standards of perfection, not your endless striving. I have waited so long to have you look up and say, 'Everything is all right when you are here.'

"I am here, Amy; I've never really left. I still want to take care of you and give you everything you need. I want you to be the person that I conceived of you to be, because I have a plan for you, and it is too wonderful for you to even imagine. I have enjoyed you because you are my precious daughter, but my delight comes from your love. I named you *Amy* because it means 'Beloved,' not because you are loved by others, but because you are loved by me."

I have summoned you by name; you are mine. . . .
Since you are precious and honored in my sight,
    and because I love you.

—Isaiah 43:1, 4

My desire now is to please my Father by obeying Him and doing His will. I want to give my heavenly Father the joy of knowing that He is enough for me. I want to daily sit in His lap and tell Him that I love Him because He delights in my love. And I want to be Daddy's girl, the girl He wants me to be.

This is my story. What will your story be? How will your life be different tomorrow than it was today? You can begin writing your story now. Where have you been and how is God changing you? Please don't put the things you've learned in this study on a shelf. Take a step of faith today to show God that you have a head that believes, a heart that is committed, and hands that are submitted to do His will. His eyes roam throughout the earth, let them fall on you. And then receive God's strength to follow Him where He leads.

I hope that you find that God is enough. He really is all that you need. He is worthy of your love, your attention, and your devotion. Let His love be the focus of your life. This is the only way to experience the abundant life He offers.

God bless you according to the wonders of His Love and may you shine!

LEADER'S GUIDE

Introduction to the Leader's Guide

If you are reading this guide, *thank you*. Thank you for investing in the lives of young women. Thank you for sacrificing your own personal time and energy so that you can have an impact on others. Thank you for your willingness to be a mentor.

This study came out of my desire to help young women experience the freedom that comes with falling out of love with the world and falling in love with Jesus Christ. The contents are primarily the product of my own personal journey combined with my experiences as a youth-pastor's wife. As all young women enter adulthood, we begin to come to grips with who we are and what we desire to become. It's my desire to see young women not waste any time before wholeheartedly serving God.

If these are your desires too, this study will help you in two areas. First, the material in *Shine* will have a personal impact on you. The most important part of being a good leader is to know yourself! Even though the material in this study was written for young women, it can impact a woman at any age. I hope that you look a little deeper into your own heart as you work through the study.

Second, *Shine* will be an effective tool, helping you to mentor your girls to grow closer to God. You are the leader and this study is *only* a tool! And a tool is only as good as the craftswoman who uses it. This tool empowers and helps you to lead your girls. It doesn't tell you how to do it. Therefore, as you go through this guide remember that all of my suggestions and questions are guidelines, not a list of "must dos." You're the expert on the young women with whom you're working because you have a relationship with them. This study in and of itself cannot mentor or disciple. In the hands of a good mentor, however, it can be a powerful discipling tool. So let the material in this study supplement and enhance your discipling relationships.

God has many blessings for those who invest a part of themselves in the lives of others. I pray that you will be blessed because of your willingness to serve Him. I am humbled and thankful that He can use me for His purposes just like He is using you.

Principles for an Effective Small Group

Leading a small group usually sounds easier than it is. Because I'm a natural born talker, I've rarely been intimidated by speaking in front of anyone. Yet, when I began leading small groups, I realized that I needed to improve a set of skills in order to maximize my effectiveness. So even if we naturally know how to talk, lead, and teach, we can all benefit by looking at ways to become great, small-group leaders. And if you feel that you're not naturally good at talking, leading, and teaching, then I'm extremely proud of you for taking on a challenge. Whatever God leads us to do, He will empower us to do it! These small-group tips will help anyone who wants to improve as a leader and facilitator.

Pray, Pray, and Pray Some More

I confess that I'm not a prayer warrior, but I hope to become one! My mother, though, is a prayer warrior and has always been an encouragement to me to grow in my prayer life. When leading a small group, it's important to pray on a weekly basis for the young women in the group. We also need to be in prayer about our own weaknesses and struggles. Satan will try to convince you that, for whatever reason, you're not capable of leading a group of girls. The best way to spiritually combat this attack is to acknowledge in prayer that you are not capable, but God is. Therefore, do not worry about anything, but pray about everything. You'll likely experience spiritual opposition and attack as you lead this small group, so prayerfully put your spiritual armor on each day.

Know the Material and Know Yourself

This may seem like stating the obvious, but the obvious sometimes needs to be stated so that we'll actually do what we know we should do. I admit that I've led a small group without familiarizing myself with the teaching. Sometimes it goes okay and sometimes I've crashed and burned. It doesn't matter how well we can lead even if we don't prepare; the point is we need to be prepared. The young women in our group deserve our best. Yet I know that on different weeks, our best may look different. The important thing is that each week we try our best to be well prepared by knowing and personally interacting with the material.

It would be optimal to have done the whole study before you lead a group through it, yet I know optimal is not usually probable. You need the time, however, to process the information in each chapter for yourself before you lead your group. Try to personally apply the material in your own life so that you'll have your own examples to share with your group.

A good small-group leader will strive, though, to keep the balance between sharing relevant personal illustrations and not sharing too much. As a leader, it's not appropriate to share personal information about which you're seeking guidance or counsel. If, for example, you're in a relationship, and you're struggling with healthy sexual boundaries, this is *not* something I'd share with girls you are mentoring. You're there to help and guide them and not to receive guidance and help. Dating dilemmas are issues you can share with your own mentor, parent, or friend. But we all struggle with sin on a daily basis, so making comments about struggling with pride or greed and asking for prayer will simply communicate to the girls in your group that you are growing just like them. The right amount of personal sharing will facilitate sharing in the group and encourage the girls to apply the information to their own lives.

Fun, Food, and Fellowship

When I led small groups, I'd regularly open the time by having some food and drinks and allowing the girls to socialize. I think it's important to have a comfortable and relaxed atmosphere. With that said, a few food tips might be helpful. Most women and girls have a love-hate relationship with food, and I try to take that into consideration when I'm leading small groups. I've been to small groups where the amount of food provided is equivalent to a dinner buffet. It's nice to provide some food but don't feel the need to go overboard. We don't want to encourage gluttony (which is a sin by the way) by creating an atmosphere that promotes overeating. So instead of having brownies, cookies, popcorn, chips, and pop, serve instead a plate of brownies and milk on one week, and then popcorn and pop on the next. We don't need to have a lot of food to create a fun atmosphere, but having a little treat makes people feel welcomed.

A short time of fellowship before you get into the study helps everyone relax, but be careful to watch the clock. It's easy to let time slip away and before you know it, you have left little time to do what you planned to do! In a small group time slot of 7:00–9:00 P.M., for example, I'd plan fellowship to go no later than 7:30 and then finish the study no later than 8:45 so that there's time to socialize at the end of the meeting. I don't like to live by time constraints, yet I know that when I follow time guidelines in my small groups, the groups simply run better.

An Atmosphere of Respect

We can't be effective small-group leaders unless we have the respect and attention of the girls in our group. Sometimes this respect is already present and sometimes we need to cultivate it. The good news is that we can cultivate an atmosphere of respect.

First of all, begin the study time with prayer. Focus on inviting the Holy Spirit to be present and to use the time to reveal God's truth. This type of prayer is helpful for you because you are reminded that you're not leading this group alone. It's also helpful for the young women in your group because it shows them that you are respecting God by submitting the time to Him. Prayer models a reverent and submissive attitude.

One leader brought to my attention that she always begins her small group with a short time of worship. I think this is an excellent way to begin the *Shine* study. You may want to use some of the songs listed in the suggested music sections, or plan some of your own. By beginning the group with prayer and then worship, you are demonstrating your dependence on and reverence for God and His Word.

Next, lay out guidelines about talking and questions in the group. Please, never allow people to talk while you are talking. If you even allow a little of this, the group will run with it. If someone talks while I'm talking, I stop until they finish or ask her to stop. If someone in your group continually does not respect you enough not to talk while you're teaching, talk quietly to that person in another room and explain to her that she will be asked to leave if she doesn't adhere to your instruction. This sort of a talk may be difficult for you to do, but if you don't address the problem, you're tolerating an atmosphere of disrespect, which will just get worse with time. It's an old rule—but one that needs to be stated and enforced—only one person can talk at a time.

Another thing to monitor during small-group discussion is tangents. Tangents are those wonderful extra stories or information that can take your group completely off the topic at hand. It's important that you as a leader keep the group talking about the material. Also, try to prevent a few people from monopolizing the conversation. Sometimes I'm the one monopolizing the conversation, and I have to reign in myself. Do your best to include everyone in the discussion.

Finally, close with prayer as a benediction to the group. Again, prayer helps us remember our dependence is on God alone.

Keep It Confidential

It's best to address the issue of confidentiality at the beginning of a small-group Bible study. No young woman wants to discuss personal issues in a group if she doesn't feel safe in doing so. It's a good idea to communicate to the participants that things shared in the group are not to leave the group. This will help facilitate an open and honest discussion. It's impossible, of course, to "guarantee" confidentiality in this type of setting, but you can strongly encourage it.

Make It Applicable

One of the biggest jobs of a leader is to make the material applicable. The easiest way to do this is to illustrate the lessons in the material with a variety of examples. You're the only one who knows the young women with whom you are working, so you have the advantage of directing your small-group discussions around the issues that are facing your own group. Try, though, not always to use the same type of examples to illustrate every point. In the chapter on idols, for example, avoid focusing on the eating-disorder example. Try using athletics or the pursuit of academic success. The impact of the material will directly relate to how well you know your girls and the issues you see them struggling with.

Format of Leader's Guide

The rest of this leader's guide is designed in a user-friendly manner. It gives you an overview of the chapter and then suggestions for your small group. The chapters in this guide consist of four divisions: the opening paragraph provides the goal of the chapter, followed by music suggestions, application questions, and additional activities.

The goal of the chapter is a summary of the main point you want the girls in your group to grasp after they've completed the lesson. To keep your discussion on topic, it's helpful to have the goal before you while you lead your group.

The music suggestions refer to songs that I've used in my own small groups and that seemed to enhance the lesson. Music often communicates to our spirits far more effectively than words alone can. Therefore, in the music section are listed some songs that can be played for your small group. You'll notice some songs are suggested for use at the beginning of the small group to serve as a discussion starter. Other songs would be better used toward the end of the night, as they symbolize the topics that were addressed in the chapter. These would serve as a good benediction just before closing with prayer. It is helpful to hand out a sheet containing the written song lyrics.

Getting music can be difficult, and certain Web sites offer music you can download for a small fee (www.itunes.com) or you can check the library. You might ask the girls in your group if they have any of the suggested music that they could bring and share with the group. Another idea is to take up a collection for the purpose of downloading the songs onto multiple CDs. That way, each girl can have something that will remind her of the study.

The application questions are to help you facilitate discussion. They are just springboards for you, and you will no doubt have your own questions that will apply to your group. The suggested questions, though, may help you get discussion started.

I've tried some of the additional activities suggested in the last division, and some have been given to me as feedback from leaders who have led groups with this material. You can use your discretion as to what might fit your group.

I certainly do not want you to feel overwhelmed. I recently read a quote that said, "Whatever is worth doing, is worth doing poorly." Don't feel like you have to use all the suggestions—or get the right music or have great food—just to lead a Bible study. If you can only do the bare bones of the study, than by all means do it. Sometimes if we wait until we can do things perfectly, we'll never do them at all. The aim for you is to joyfully lead your small group through this material. If you're doing something with joy, you're doing a great job!

1

The World Around Us

Shine Like a Star

The goal of this chapter is to help girls see that the messages with which they're bombarded on a daily basis are not neutral. By the end of the chapter, they should begin to recognize that Satan is the author of many of the trends we see in culture. They should also take away from this chapter that God's ways are not always obvious to us and His path for our lives requires us to be alert and seek His ways out in this world.

Music Suggestions

- "Shine" by Newsboys (from *Shine*)
  This is an excellent song to use to begin your first group. The words in the chorus effectively describe the goal of this study: to shine for God. You might want to ask the girls how they currently "shine" for God and what they would like to gain from this study.

- "Damascus Road" by Rich Mullins (from *Brother's Keeper*)
  The lyrics of "Damascus Road" make it a good theme song for this chapter. However, many young women may not enjoy the style of music. This song may be played at the beginning of the lesson because it can help facilitate discussion. You can ask specific questions about the song such as, "What do you think the songwriter means when he

sings, 'You took away the mask of life, they had placed upon the face of death'?"

• "Visions" by Jennifer Knapp (from *Kansas*)
I've included many Jennifer Knapp songs in this study because she's one of my favorite artists, and I find her lyrics to have depth and insight. In this song she talks about desiring heaven over this world. She uses the phrase, "They say I am much too demanding to want a better place than here." This song works well to close the lesson, or even to use in the middle of the lesson as a springboard for talking about the craziness of this world and how we should all want to see more of heaven in our own lives.

Application Questions

1. Can you relate to any of the three common traps referred to in the lesson? Can you give an example of when you might have fallen into one of the three traps?
2. How do the media, your friends, and the culture you live in influence your thinking?
3. First John 5:19 could be translated, "The whole world lies in bed with the Evil One." What does this image mean to you?
4. Can you recall a time when you've taken your cues on how to behave or think from the world instead of from God?
5. Can you give any examples of how you see Satan at work in the world around you? You can elaborate on ideas in the text or come up with your own examples.
6. Have you ever thought about God's specific plan for your life?

Additional Activities

You might bring, or have the girls bring in, some popular teen magazines and use them to illustrate Satan's influence over our culture. You may also wish to consider taping a popular TV show (but make sure it's appropriate!) and watch a portion of the show as a group to analyze the kind of messages that may come from the show. If you decide to do so, be sure to plan the segment of the show ahead of time and personally watch it before you show it.

You may also wish to have the group read "The Road Too Often Taken" illustration from the chapter, having each girl read a segment. After it's been read, ask for personal reactions to the analogy.

2

The Child Within Us

The Real You

The aim of this chapter is to help each girl trust Christ with her identity. The difference between understanding who you are in Christ and truly believing who you are in Christ is the essential component of the chapter. We want them to see that it's not easy to truly believe God and that it requires courage. The group members should recognize that true belief in God is evidenced by a change in attitudes and behaviors.

Music Suggestions

- "Creed" by Rich Mullins (from *A Liturgy, a Legacy, and a Ragamuffin Band;* also performed by Third Day on *Offerings II: All I Have to Give*) This song can be played at the end of the session to reinforce the message of the chapter. Use your discretion, however—you may feel it would be more helpful at the beginning. A good lyric to bring to the group's attention is, "I did not make it but it is making me." This statement illustrates that we are the product of our beliefs and that what we believe truly does make us who we are. If you do play it at the beginning of the group it should be played again at the end as a benediction.

- "Voice of Truth" by Casting Crowns (from *Casting Crowns*)
  This song is illustrative of how we need to listen to God's voice above all the other voices of the world, and works well at the end of the session.

- "Child of Mine" by Mark Schulz (from *Stories and Songs*)
  This song communicates the importance of believing that we are God's children.

Application Questions

1. What was your reaction to reading the identity in Christ list?
2. Before reading this chapter, how would you say your identity in Christ affected your daily attitudes, emotions, and behaviors?
4. What have you learned that may assist you in making your identity in Christ have an impact on you every day?
5. What do you think the Bible means when it says that Mary was blessed for believing God?
6. How do you think you would be blessed by God for believing what He says is true of you?

Additional Activities

The following example is a good illustration of what it means to put your faith in God. You may want to use this during your group.

Wheelbarrow Example: There was once a famous tightrope walker who took the challenge of walking on a tightrope across Niagara Falls. Before he set out, he asked the audience to raise their hands if they believed he could make it across the falls. No one in the crowd raised his or her hand. The tightrope walker made it across the falls and back.

After he'd finished, he told the crowd that he was now going to walk across the falls and push a wheelbarrow. He asked the crowd again if anyone believed that he could make it across. Again, no one in the crowd raised his or her hand. And once again, the man met his challenge and crossed the tightrope back and forth while pushing a wheelbarrow.

When he finished, the crowd was amazed and cheered like crazy. The man had one last challenge. He asked, "How many of you think that I could walk on this tightrope pushing the wheelbarrow with a person in it?" At this the hands of the entire crowd went up because they were so impressed with what he'd already done. The crowd shouted, "We believe you can do it!" The man then asked, "Okay, who wants to get in the wheelbarrow?" All the hands went down.

Ask the girls if they've "gotten into the wheelbarrow" when it comes to believing God.

3

American Idol(s)

Who's on the Throne?

The main objectives in chapter 3 are to identify idols in our hearts and to discover how these idols have robbed us of some of God's blessings. By the end of this week, the young women in your group should have a deeper understanding of what it means to trust God with their whole hearts.

Music Suggestions

- "Faithful to Me" by Jennifer Knapp (from *Kansas*)
  This song directly communicates about the worthlessness of idols. Make sure to use the version at the end of the CD because it has a

second verse. Playing it at the beginning of the lesson will encourage group discussion; playing it again at the end is a nice prelude to the closing prayer.

- "Whole Again" by Jennifer Knapp (from *Kansas*)
  This song works well at the end of the lesson because it addresses the issue of giving our whole hearts to God.

- "Love Song for a Savior" by Jars of Clay (from *Jars of Clay*)
  This is a poetic song that gracefully communicates the desire to fall in love with Jesus, which is what we all need to do in order to abandon idols in our hearts.

Application Questions

1. Have the girls take a few moments to write down any idols they've constructed in their own hearts. As the girls are encouraged to explore their own idols, it should be emphasized that the list of idols in the chapter is not exhaustive.
2. Have a time of sharing about their idols, but members of the group shouldn't feel pressured to share if they are uncomfortable.
3. Ask the group what they have gained from worshipping, bowing down, serving, and sacrificing to their idols? What have they lost?
4. Ask the group to speculate on how their lives might be different if they took the time, energy, and resources they gave to their idols and instead gave it to God.
5. Discuss the difference between enjoying something in your life versus having it become an idol.
6. Ask the group if it's possible that God might have us give up something that is good for us (not just bad things) if it's holding the wrong place in our hearts. Ask for examples.

Additional Activities

One of the most difficult issues in this chapter is distinguishing be-tween idols and things that we enjoy. We don't want any girl leaving the session thinking that shopping is wrong, having a boyfriend is wrong, exercise is wrong, etc.

If it's possible, it would be excellent to show a clip from the movie *Chariots of Fire*. I would pick a clip that directly related to what Eric Liddle sacrificed in order to obey God and how God blessed him. Contrast the life of Eric Liddle with this advertisement for the Chicago Marathon that was on the radio a few years ago: "Tomorrow [the day of the marathon] the road to salvation is twenty-six miles long." Discuss how the radio ad represents that exercise is becoming an idol in someone's life.

4

Lies from the Dark Side

Follow the Light

The goal of chapter 4 is to reveal the lies that we have believed deep within our hearts. These lies will often correspond with the idols that were identified in chapter 3. By the end of this week, the girls should have a grasp of certain lies they believe and how these lies affect their everyday lives. They should also have an understanding that the only way to combat the lies is with the active application of God's truth in their hearts. They should recognize that they are in a war and that they need to stand firm and fight.

Music Suggestions

- "I Live to Know You" by Hill Songs Australia (from *All Things Are Possible*)
  This song works well at the end of the lesson as a closing prayer. The line in the song, "And His kingdom is established as I live to know You more," can be explained that as God's truth is revealed in our lives it not only benefits us, but it also establishes more of God's light in this world. The "light of the world" passage in Matthew 5:14–16 would make an appropriate closing Scripture before playing the song.

- "Clay and Water" by Margaret Becker (from *Falling Forward*)
  This song is a little abstract, but this is a good time in the study to introduce the idea that as you follow God's truth, you are actually becoming more yourself. A lyric in the song, "Slowly I am becoming who I am," depicts the process of this study.

Application Questions

1. Ask the girls which items on the list they agree are lies and whether they see some things on the list that don't appear to be lies. This can be a heated discussion, and two points need to be reiterated:

   a. The lies on the list are not necessarily universal. For example, "I need to exercise every day," is a lie for the girl who has made exercise or her body an idol in her life. Someone may respond that she's on a sports team and is required to exercise every day. Explain that exercise is not an idol unless being in the sport in and of itself has become an idol. If the sport is an idol, that doesn't necessarily mean that she cannot be in the sport, but this study may cause her to reevaluate the priority that the sport has in her heart.

   b. Some girls will argue that statements such as, "I'm not attractive," are true for some people. If so, bring them back to the lesson in chapter 1. A good response to that argument is to ask the question, "Whose rules do you want to live by—Satan's or God's?" In this discussion, the girls need continually to be reminded that Christ set them free from Satan's rules. Look up Galatians 5:1: "It is for freedom that Christ has set us free. Stand firm, then, and do not let yourselves be burdened again by a yoke of slavery."

2. Have the girls break into smaller groups for the "Lies and Truth Worksheets." You can assign lies if they don't want to choose a lie themselves.
3. Discuss first as a group the lies entered in the "lies" portion of the worksheets, and then assign to them God's truth for each lie. Talk about how believing God's truth would change their everyday lives.
4. It's helpful to assign them homework for the week in which they are encouraged to do the lie and truth worksheets. Always encourage them to write down their responses because it helps them to see their thoughts on paper.

Additional Activities

Ask the girls to read the passage in Ephesians 6 about the armor of God. You may wish to have each girl in the group read a verse. Having them underline all the action verbs in the passage illustrates that this Scripture is not in the passive voice but is calling for action from the believer. Talk about the spiritual battle we face in applying God's truth in our lives, and ask the young women for examples of spiritual battles they are currently facing.

5

Living in Submission
Trust and Obey

The point of this chapter is to teach the role of submission and obedience in our lives. The girls should have an understanding that God places visible people in authority over us in this world as practice for submitting to the invisible God. They should also realize that in surrendering to God's will we find the most happiness, peace, and contentment.

Music Suggestions

- "Hands in the Air" by The Waiting (from *Waiting*)
  This is a rather lengthy song that tells about a person who's in a battle of dying to his own self-will and then finding liberation in doing so. The song works best when used toward the middle of the lesson. You could introduce the subject and have some discussion about submission and obedience, and then play the song before talking about dying to one's will. I think many girls will enjoy analyzing the lyrics of this song.

- "Deliver Me" by Margaret Becker (from *Falling Forward*)
  This poetic song talks about the need to be delivered from ourselves. It works well at the end of the lesson before prayer.

- "The Wonderful Cross" by Chris Tomlin (from *The Noise We Make*)
  This is a popular worship piece that we often sing, but may not grasp the meaning of the words. The song speaks of dying so that we can live. You could talk about how we have to die to our own wants and desires when we choose to live in submission and obedience.

Application Questions

1. Ask the group for their responses to this statement: "Satan will deceive us into believing that we can be disobedient and disrespectful to the authorities in our lives yet still have a submissive heart toward God."
2. Have you ever thought of Jesus learning to be obedient?
3. How does this change the way you view Jesus' willingness to die on the cross for you?
4. What do you think about the connection between loving God and obeying God?
5. How many examples can you think of in nature that illustrate the principle of new life after death (e.g., the seasons, the sun setting and rising, the process of becoming a butterfly)?
6. What do you think is meant by the statement, "There is no comfortable alternative to God's will." Do you think you might be guilty of exploring comfortable alternatives to God's will?

Additional Activities

You may wish to return to media examples of how society almost always paints people in authority in a negative light. Students, for example, are more intelligent than their teachers, children are wiser than their parents, and animals are smarter than humans. It's not difficult to find movies and TV shows that model the idea that children have more wisdom than their parents or other adults. At an earlier point in the study, it might be interesting to poll the girls in your group about what are some of their favorite movies and TV shows. Then you could bring in a clip or a few clips that demonstrate how they are bombarded with the idea that they know more than their elders. Usually these clips will also provide examples of disrespect to elders and parents, which is now so commonplace in our culture.

6

Loving by Doing

The JOY of the Lord

The goal of this chapter is to express that our spiritual growth will be evidenced by our growth in love. Our love for God and our love for others will increase as we grow closer to Christ in our walk with Him. The girls should recognize the role that emotions can play in our lives and how feelings can mislead us. They should also come to realize that loving God and others first will lead to more joy in their own lives.

Music Suggestions

- "Make Me an Instrument" by Ragamuffin Band (from *Prayers of a Ragamuffin*)
  I highly recommend this song, so if you can get it, please do! It's an uplifting and inspirational conclusion to this study, and works well at the end of the session. You may wish to discuss the lyrics of the song before playing it.

- "Choose Life" by Big Tent Revival (from *Choose Life*)
  As a benediction at the end of the session this song addresses our deciding between God's ways and the world's ways.

- "Hero" by Superchick (from *Last One Picked*)
  This is a good song especially for younger audiences, although I'm not young and I like it a lot. It talks about how you can be a hero by showing God's love.

- "Legacy" by Nicole Nordeman (from *Woven and Spun*)
  I love this song too! This works well as a benediction because it gets

the young women thinking about how they would like to be remembered. Will they be remembered for winning others to God, or for winning people to themselves? This is a good song to use as the girls are now almost graduates of the study.

Application Questions

1. How do you typically measure your own spiritual growth? Are any of these ways wrong? Have them explain their answers.
2. What do you think are the major obstacles when it comes to loving God and loving others?
3. Can you give an example of a time when you trusted your feelings and you found out they weren't so trustworthy?
4. How do our emotions both help and enhance our walk with Christ? How can they be a hindrance?
5. What are some examples you learned about love in your childhood that you may unknowingly dismiss now?
6. How do these ideas relate to Jesus' comments about becoming a child to enter the kingdom of heaven?

Additional Activities

You might have each member of the group write down the name of a person in her life whom she finds very difficult to love. Ask each girl to commit to praying for that person. Also, have each girl pray that God would give her love for that person, in spite of her negative feelings. Encourage the girls to pray for each other and keep each other accountable; they can ask each other how they're doing at praying for the individual about whom they're having negative feelings.

Conclusion

He Is Enough

I've written my own personal testimony as a conclusion to this study. It might be helpful for you, as the group leader, to write and share your own story. The girls in your group may feel some connection with me, but they are far more connected to you. Therefore, the more you share of yourself, the more of a lasting impact or legacy you will have on them. It takes extra time as you write out your own testimony, but I think you'll find it a worthwhile experience for you and the young women you're serving.

Thank God for People Like You

I hope you've enjoyed the *Shine* study and that it's been an enriching experience for you and the young women you've been leading. Thank you again for all the time, energy, and love you have put into the young women you are discipling. Studies like this cannot have any real impact without people like you. I pray that you will be blessed in ways you cannot imagine, and may you always continue to grow in your relationship with the God who loves you. You are precious and honored in His sight.

God's an Artist and You're a Masterpiece

0-8254-3467-X

Did you know . . . .

> The human brain can store as much information as a 500-mile-long row of books? Earth's moon weighs 81 quintillion tons—a lightweight by space standards? The sun is so big that over one million Earths could fit inside it?

> We take in about 23,000 breaths a day, which amounts to 630 million in an average lifetime?

Today, so many people question whether or not there is a God. On the other hand, many people believe in Him but don't know why. In *God's an Artist and You're a Masterpiece*, Lorraine Peterson brings scientific truths and personal narratives together to show us that there really is a Creator, and that He is a loving God with a plan for our lives.

Dear Diary . . .

Jana's Journal
0-8254-4117-X

> "I stood on that street corner for maybe as long as it took to count to five. It was all happening so fast! There wasn't time to think, and my head spun with trying to make a decision."
> —excerpt from *Jana's Journal*

Jana Thompson had high hopes for her last year of high school. She had dreamt about what her senior year would look like, but after the first few days of school, all those dreams seemed to crumble to the ground. Things could get really messy as Jana deals with a brutal self-image problem, a desperately cute guy with an exasperating commitment to the community, an encounter with an inner-city gang, and a family she would love to wish on her worst enemy. Could it get any worse? Sneak a peek at *Jana's Journal*—it's going to be a wild ride!